6S

SIX SENTENCES

Volume 2

Copyright © 2009 by Robert McEvily

All rights reserved. No part of *Six Sentences, Volume 2* may be reproduced or transmitted in any form or by any means, electronic or mechanical, including photocopying, recording, or by any information storage and retrieval system, without permission in writing from the copyright owner.

Six Sentences, Volume 2 was printed in the United States of America.

What can *you* say in six sentences?

sixsentences.blogspot.com

CONTENTS

Introduction by Neil LaBute 9

Part 1 15

Part 2 59

Part 3 103

Part 4 145

Part 5 187

Part 6 225

Bonus Section 259

About the Authors 267

Author Blogs and Websites 291

The Hidden Message 301

The Final Page 302

for Jill

Introduction

by Neil LaBute

"Hell, anybody can do this."

That might be your first thought when you sit down to tackle the dilemma that is "Six Sentences."

Then it begins to weigh on you ~ what to write, what to say, how can I make this stand out from all the others while still being brilliant and clever and worldly and funny and sexy and moving and, let's face it, the best?

I came to this process a skeptic but I remain because of its pure and simple joys ~ the stark, primal beauty of words on a page (or at least the electronic equivalent of), the euphoria that always seems to build as you begin to write again, and the blunt satisfaction of finishing something that you can proudly post and force your friends (if you're so lucky as to have any) to read or at least pretend to be aware of.

It's so easy to judge; it's easy to be a critic ~ which means it's easy to be a parasite ~ but much, much harder to actually take up the pen or keyboard and slice open a literary vein with it, spilling yourself out for all to see and read and mock and maybe even learn from, so to all of you "bloggers" and "six sentence armchair quarterbacks" out there, I say, "go on, go ahead, give it a try, let's see what *you* can do if it's so damn easy."

I double dare you.

Those Who Took the Double Dare

(in 6 parts)

Part 1

Six Questions

by Rick Moody

Once had a love, once, once; once had a love, once, once, once, an only love, once, an only love, once, once, once; if I had a love, was it an only love, or did I once have a love that was more, more than an only love, did once I have a love that was more than an only love, a once love, a more than once love, or was it more than that once? More than once, more than love, more than only, more than, than, than what? More than what kind of thing, because is there only one kind of thing, one kind of love, or are there more kinds than one, and would I be lonely, if there were just the one kind, and are kinds of love, can you discuss kinds of love, or would it be among the kindnesses of love to refrain from a discussion of kinds of love, love bold, love slight, love curmudgeonly, love lost, love profane, these being assembled, in some database of love? And who's doing the loving, after all, word known to all men, or is it a condition of the world to have once had a love, in a twilight setting, wandering and using the past tense, the first-person conveys such a reassuring past tense and lost tense, that it very nearly becomes okay to write six questions on such a sentimental topic ~ I have six questions about love, and does that make me a lover, and does it make me a protagonist or a narrator, is it inevitable that a narrator has to narrate a story that starts "once had a love," or can there be a lost love like there is a tree in the woods, and thus that lost love is like a gentle mist rolling on a British countryside, summoning, in its absence a desperate but well-educated British woman who is a crack seamstress, but unmarried at the ripe old age of 23, and who needs a man with a certain income, even if he has a mad first wife secreted in a barn or attic? And of what kind of lost love would that woman write, the one in the attic, not the one who is the crack seamstress, of loves lonely and unfulfilled, of passions quenched and unquenched, or kinks unremarked upon in the novels of the past? Does it make her the protagonist, who thinks there was once a boy, and was once a classroom, and was once a discussion of English grammar, and was once a breakfast of watery oatmeal, and at each of these there was a love, or perhaps a pang of love, if such a thing can be spoken of, a pang, and for each pang, there was a self, but a self that existed in a group, because the desire did not have a desire until it had a group into which it fitted the desire, and the thwarting of desire, the layering over of desire was a thing to be wished for, with prayers and imprecations and repetitions, oh, I wish, I wish, I devoutly wish, I fervently, I desire and I wish not to desire, I desire not to desire, just this once, so as not to have a lack of a love, or a love that is no longer a lover, or an object of love that is no longer a love that once love, nor a love that is, but a love that might be in the future, or a desire that might be, so that, after all there is a way out of the attic, or the barn, or the basement ~ a love that is to come?

The Brightness of the Awful Year

by Amy Guth

The year, particularly the autumn and first tinges of winter, was an awful one. The last months of the year, when the days shortened and the cold darkness shook leaves from trees and chilled the entirety of nature into stillness until spring, threatened to topple the days years ago that Sarah held as a watermark for the worst, the bottom, the very greatest that she was capable of suffering. Alone, with snow swirling around her and falling onto her eyelashes and outstretched fingertips, Sarah considered all of this on New Year's Eve, and with the old gilded cuckoo clock gingerly laid in the snow beside her feet, as it hummed out a soothing tick-tick-tick as the year came to an end, she felt relieved to see the year go, as if the quiet act of seeing it off ensured the end to the dark luck that whispered at her feet all autumn. Sarah considered what unbearableness could possibly ever overtake that winter as the most terrible she hoped to ever see, and thought again of the dark luck and a sudden thought struck her, a thought so wild and unimaginable that she felt hot and shivery inside as it coursed through her. The idea leaked into Sarah's thoughts with a song, a song for which she felt so deeply during the bad winter, a song she loved but hadn't sought to hear since that winter, and she felt the song again, as deeply as she did all those years ago. The song snaked through her mind and Sarah realized the dark winter was lessened somehow for finding this song again, as the tiny, sacred act of loving this bright moment, a discarded scrap of shining comfort, a beautiful something leftover from that aching time, that awful winter all those years ago, healed her and held her and Sarah felt wonderfully far away from those days.

Masks

by Joseph Grant

No one is ever truly happy. No one is ever truly ever anything. Whatever one is, there is usually another emotion, lying just beneath the surface, an undercurrent of the real stormy sea that rages within, ready to flood the shores of one's life when the daylight became a muttered curse and the nights became blacker than Hell. We all wear masks to hide our true identity; our true emotions, depending on with whom we are interacting. Jack watched across the way as a girl he once went to college with was loudly explaining to her boyfriend how he would have to get another job now that she was pregnant and Jack noticed how the guy looked back at her with a shocked and bemused smile that hid the emotion of his inner panic and indignation the guy was clearly suppressing. She had always wanted a child since he could remember back at school, she must have, he smiled wickedly, given the amount of endless guys with whom she had slept. She wore a different mask now, never to let this one drop, as she would never tell the guy that the baby wasn't his.

Breakfast with Billy the Kid

by Brian Steel

If there's one matter I can relate to you with some authority, it's that ham and eggs are better enjoyed when you're not getting robbed at gunpoint. One morning I was sitting in the Café on the Route in the lovely little town of Baxter Springs, Kansas, having just ordered another glass of freshly-squeezed orange juice when my breakfast companion, the illustrious Professor Barnabus, informed me of the fact that the very establishment we were enjoying our breakfast in was, in fact, never meant to be in the business of supplying gastronomic sustenance at all, but had, for the longest time, been known in these parts simply as, "The Bank That Billy The Kid Robbed." At first I thought of it as no more than a humorous prevarication on my colleague's part, but as I casually observed the interior architectural features of the place: the high ceiling, the noble, Neo-Classical columns by the entrance, and the old outlines of bank teller cages, separating the diners from the kitchen, it began to dawn on me that this, in fact, was not one of the Professor's infamous "practical jokes" but one of his lesser-known "actual" historical anecdotes, and the more I looked around, the more the café began to transform before me into an old, western-style, oak-paneled bank. In fact, the more I stared at our busboy, the more the teenager's thin, wispy mustache became a bushy handlebar, the more I noticed the scar along his cheek and the slight, limping gait, and when he asked (rather aggressively, I might add) if I was done with my dishes, I raised my hands and screamed, "Take it all Billy, just leave me breathing!" Just then, as if the previous confrontation hadn't been terrifying enough, the doors swung open and what I remember briefly as a family of five quickly melted into the James Gang; their baseball caps became dark and low-brimmed cowboy hats caked with dust, their camera straps became bandoliers, fanny packs transformed into imposing belt buckles, and what was once a small cell phone, held by the father, became the gleaming, silver body of a Colt .45, cocked and ready to use in the cracked, leathery hands of Jesse himself. I gave up all pretense of bravery or nobility and dove to the ground, crawling out the front door before the invariable shots rang out, shattering the peaceful morning air into a million broken shards, my long-distant memories of ham and eggs and a second glass of orange juice now left a thousand miles behind, in Baxter Springs, Kansas; a dusty, little town where, I, for one, shall never dare return.

Random Generator

by Megan Monserez

"Isn't it weird, the way they just patch the sentences together from some computer bank of temperatures and conditions?" you asked, your gaze never straying from the Weather Channel as the robotic voice predicted in its familiar, stilted way the week ahead. "They don't even try to make the forecasts sound like they aren't just a bunch of common phrases cobbled together. But I guess it wouldn't make sense for someone to record unique sentences every time - I mean, there's only so many ways for the weather to go, and only so many ways to say so." And I knew you were right those months later, when the refrains of "I think we should see other people," "you deserve better than this," and "it's not you, it's me" spurted from your lips in one non sequitur after another, as if you had pulled them at random out of a hat, or run a program to computer-generate our breakup. Though I did at the time, I can't really blame you for that: there are, after all, only so many ways for things to happen, and there's a kindness in not inventing cruelly-specific new ways to explain them. Even so, I closed the door gently to keep your tropes on the other side, cocooned into the blankets, and turned the dial to the chief meteorologist at Channel 5.

Dooley Noted

by Harry B. Sanderford

All morning long his nerves had been on edge and he couldn't shake the feeling he was being watched. He had a clean line of sight six miles in any direction and right now as far as he could see, he and his mule Katie were the only two in the territory. Dooley stopped the bottle and slid it back in his saddlebag, admonishing himself for being so damn jumpy. He gave Katie her reins to roll a smoke and was licking the gummed paper when he heard a soft snap and turned in its direction. A nearly imperceptible imperfection at first, an eyelash viewed in peripheral vision became a stitch on the horizon and then a seam unraveling an opening in the fabric of the sky. Dooley looked up to see the clear blue winking open to reveal a world size bloodshot eye, grabbed himself a handful of reins and slapping Katie's flanks had a little chuckle and shouted, "Well on the upside Katie, at least we ain't goin' crazy!"

You Know Them

by Lauren Becker

Ballerina girls. No stains on white shirts. No tripping on stairs. No dishes in sinks. No bruises on hips. No star wishes for grace.

Flyover Country

by Eugenia E. Gratto

Just after the movie on my Christmas Eve flight from San Francisco to Chicago, I raised the windowshade to look at the snow-swept plains below. A year earlier, I drove those roads, which were hateful when snow and sleet fell, but so beautiful on an afternoon like the one I was flying through, when orange light from the setting sun caught fire to the snow and the tiny buildings alongside the roads. "I'm not *from* Iowa," I tell the Californians. And it's true. But my time in that state was so wonderful and so awful at the same time, such a mix of pleasure and friends and crazy discoveries ~ about plants, cooking, myself ~ and of one of the darkest depressions I've ever experienced, a bitter depression that required physical and emotional thawing, that it will always be a place marked on my body, my heart, in a way very few places in my life ever have been before. And so, as I flew over Iowa on my way to Chicago, I appreciated that fire-on-snow, those hard corners in the roads carved through the white, the small towns bleeding into the prairie from intersections.

An Insensitive Prick

by Joe Lo Truglio

I watched a friend's four-year-old kid play drums to Squeeze's "Up the Junction" the other day. He didn't miss a beat – bonafide prodigy. How come a tot can self-teach tricky upbeats, but a 39-year-old waitress in Crystal River can't remember to bring me a salad? I'll tell you how come. One's a genius and the other's working at a horribly understaffed Denny's rip-off with bad management. (See, and you guys thought I was going to be an insensitive prick.)

Poetry Workshop 501

by Sean Patrick Hill

Three hundred and sixty three thousand five hundred and eighty two twenty-three-year-olds applied for the "graduatecreativewritingprogram" where the best of the best were chosen, and the rest went back to work as baristas. For the next two years, the best of the best paid their tuition with variable-interest student loans and sat in the room on couches and read from their works of genius. One wrote an experimental poem about a pair of socks and a serial killer and everyone in the room lauded its brilliant capacity for image and voice; another wrote a poem as if the letters were alphabet soup, and she was praised for her impressive range. The professor talked about important things like discursiveness, avoiding sentimentality and other irrational feelings, not to mention Lorine Niedekker's contribution to the postmodern aesthetic. They sent their poems to online journals that lasted, on average, seventeen weeks and applied for grants and won first-book awards judged by geriatrics. They graduated and were given pieces of paper and joined the burgeoning work force as highly educated baristas.

Bailey

by Kevin Michaels

On a sidewalk near Vesey Street, Bailey shook his cup and smiled at each person as he asked for spare change. Dreadlocked and dirty, the sores on his arms covered by long sleeves, he tried hiding the shame in his eyes while ignoring the occasional taunts of "get a job you fucking bum." Even though he was used to it the words always hurt, almost as much as the sneers businessmen gave him and the way women stuffed coins back in their purses, turning cold shoulders to him as if he were invisible. Inside Starbucks the Assistant Manager started towards the door again to chase him away; Bailey was hurrying to put his belongings back in his cart when the first plane slammed in the Tower. Within hours the neighborhood that he knew had drastically changed – those same men and women now looked just like him with dazed expressions and blank stares, afraid and fearful of all they had lost. And in the horror of that day, when it all fell apart for so many, Bailey smiled as he realized that for once he wasn't alone with his fears any more.

Boy Met Girl

by Whitney Pastorek

Boy met Girl under the ferris wheel one sunlit summer's day. There they stayed—feet together, side by side, not quite breathing—for what seemed like forever before anyone spoke. "You are everything I want," said Boy to Girl, his blue eyes unmoved from the ride as his blue heart begged her to believe him. "I believe you," she said, though her head, too, did not turn. The ferris wheel spun; their hands fell from their pockets and moved inch by inch ever closer until they found themselves standing with fingers interlaced, hope held tight between their palms. At a nearby midway stand, the siren rang, and a barker yelled "Winner!" into the spotless sky.

Adherence

by Stephen J. Davis

I really wanted to learn Spanish to charm my Latin girlfriend into having sex with me. I figured a label maker would help develop my vocabulary so I used one to identify the translation of everything, from sticking ESPEJO on my mirror to LECHE on my milk. Mariana couldn't help but be flattered, "¡Eres tan dulce!" she said. But my vocabulary thirst wasn't quenched just yet, "¿Cómo se dice 'neck' en español?" I asked. With her answer, I printed out a label then attached it to her skin. Resistant at first ("¡Que cosquillas!"), she eventually welcomed a label for every detail of her body, until finally, I became bilingual.

The Smart Moose

by Tao Lin

In a small forest in Alaska a moose sharpens its antlers on a glacier. The moose cuts down five trees with its antlers and builds a canoe. The moose carries the canoe and beats a group of campers with it killing eight children, two adults, and an Inuit passerby. The moose cries. The moose lays in a fetal position in the canoe. A few days later the canoe arrives in Japan where for the last eighteen years the moose has been general manager at the Kyoto headquarters of Sony's ear piece department.

Slice

by L. Allison Stein

It was too late, and as the keys jingled their way into the front door's lock, Amy's palms started to grow moist. The knife slid, easy enough, from her grasp, but remained lodged upright, awkward; a beacon of the crime she had just committed. Her thoughts waded slowly through the slush of fear and the shame of being caught, and around the base of the protruding blade, a thick, dark substance began to ooze. The sound of the door opening sent Amy's hand to her head, wiping at the sweat on her brow with dripping palms, echoed by armpits that itched with rising anxiety. There was no getting out of this one, that was for sure; her perfectly toned, stud of a husband would come through the door, home from the gym, find her at the kitchen table, and that would conclude any mal nutritious affair she hadn't even had a chance to start; guilty as charged. *Well, fuck it,* Amy's brain said as she dug her fingers into the gooey body of the chocolate cake that lay before her, and when she shoved the moist deliciousness into her mouth, she began to giggle.

Lighting Candles for Martyrs

by Arsalan Pirzada

It takes a lot to evoke empathy in these times, when everyone is so desensitized by television gunshots and the Kabul syndrome. When empathy comes, it doesn't break you or hurt you, it just dissolves all compassion. Then you forget all the light-a-candles and the barbecues and gala dinners for charity. You don't have an opinion anymore, you don't care. People die, they always have, and that's life. A journey of empathy wrapped in callousness.

Some Have Meaning

by Alyssa Quintieri

Those words have bounced around in my head since they were spoken. When I was very young, people would say to me (but mostly to, or for, my mother), "She's going to be a heartbreaker." I'd get so angry, naively unaware of the statement being a compliment. I took offense to it, thinking, "Why do they think that about me? Why do they think I will break boys' hearts?" Life slows down and sometimes comes to an achingly slow crawl before it shocks your system completely and love fills everyone's hearts.

New Leaf

by Christen Buckler

Surrounded by expensive healthy food, I walk down the cereal aisle and there she is: Lycra top, midriff showing, full makeup, hair done, reading a box of granola bars because she can only afford so many calories a day. And a little girl in pigtails and purple plaid walks beside me, looking at things above her head and above her budget. The hairdo lady makes *the face*: the face says *you're worthless, you're annoying, you're not worth half of what I am*. I get angry and I get hateful, and all I can think is: at least wait until this little girl is thirteen (fourteen, maybe) and the sugar & spice has been replaced by vinegar & piss, and she'll hate her mama and her daddy and hate you and your mascara eyes and be able to hand you that sneer right back. Just wait until you get *the face* aimed in your direction and you'll know that not all little girls grow up to be perfect & poised like you. But they're the ones I like much more anyway.

Our Country in Darkness

by David Barringer

An American owl hooted in a fallen night. Caught by the frost, young Marion booted alone around the moonlit house, fingering the engagement ring from the boy, now killed, in the empty room of her big coat pocket, and then braced herself and secured the cellar door. Stags shouldered into the decimated forest, snow on the blackened ash of limbs, steam from nostrils sighing with hunger. Inside, Marion's younger sister Clare warmed into her bruises, dried the clothes of their drowned mother Elizabeth by the choking furnace, left off stabbing the floorboards to tighten a screw with the point of the knife. Their father Arthur was a fisherman, a drunk, a failure, and worse. Left hanging in his own skin, his heart lynched from the branches of his ribs, Arthur pleaded in town for something useful to be asked of him.

Six Days to Sundown

by Brenda J. Gannum

He slipped the six new bullets into the spinner of his six-shooter and stuffed it into his holster. Unlashing his horse from the rail in front of the Triple Six Saloon, he mounted quickly and headed off toward Six Skulls Gulch, hoping to find the six desperados who had raped his wife six nights before. Six different witnesses assured him that was their secret hangout, and he figured he could make the 66-mile journey over the rough terrain in under six hours. Sixty miles west of town, crossing the abandoned tracks of the old 666 Express from Carson City, his horse stumbled on a loose rail and broke his foreleg. There was nothing else to do but put him down, even though he would have to waste one of the six bullets that he was saving for his mission. Six days later, with the sun beating down, the water in his canteen gone, and delirium setting in, he stared in disbelief as the buzzards – exactly six of them – began their ominous circling.

Traveling to the Moon on a Budget

by Adam J. Whitlatch

When I was a little boy, about nine or ten, I built my own spacesuit. It was a rather crude looking thing, being made mostly from old dryer vent hoses and my father's scuba gear, but over time the design became much more elaborate as I began adding such necessities as pressure gaskets, seals, and asbestos insulation; by the time I was fifteen I was certain that I could safely walk on the moon - or, gee whiz, even *Mars* - in my homemade spacesuit, but *getting there* was the problem. I remember reading somewhere that by the year 2000 there would be human colonies on the moon and even commercial flights between the Earth and its lone natural satellite complete with complimentary peanuts and an in-flight movie; these flights were going to be expensive, so naturally I needed money. So I did the next logical thing. . . I got a job, or -more accurately - I got three jobs: an early morning newspaper route, in the summer I mowed lawns, and after school I flipped burgers at the local diner until nine o'clock. It was on one of these hot July nights when I was riding my bike home, covered in the stink of hamburger grease, that I came upon the strange craft parked in the center of Van Buren Street and the tall, skinny silver man silhouetted in the blinding light radiating from inside the craft beckoned to me, urging me closer. I suppose I should have been frightened - shucks, anyone in their right mind would have been - but a grin spread across my young, blemished face as I remembered the crude homemade spacesuit hanging from a coat hook in my bedroom closet and called out to the pilot of the shimmering craft, "Don't go away... I'll be *right* back!"

Rehearsal

by Valerie O'Riordan

When I was in school, we'd go around wearing meaningful friendship bracelets on both wrists, and our nails would be painted at least two different colours at any given time. For a few months, the 'in thing' was to paint this thick gunk called hair mascara in blue or pink streaks all over your head. The younger kids loved us. We'd go out on a Saturday wearing tight trousers and drink toxic pink alco-pops down the back of a local pub which mainly catered to people that weren't allowed into the classier joints out on the main road. We'd draw our eyes into shape with cunning pencils, and make cheekbones out of nothing, and talk our way into R-Rated movies, and pretend we knew exactly what was going on. Everyone had everyone else fooled.

Information

by Bob Heman

The carrot and the stick are usually paired. Traditionally if you are good you are given a carrot and if you are bad you get the stick. The carrot might only be a compliment or a kind word or small favor, the stick a silence or criticism or mild rebuke. Sometimes the stick may be her anger and the carrot her comforting embrace. Within a relationship the carrot may be a sexual favor she has not usually granted, and the stick a physical punishment she gives to change his attitude or selfish behavior. In these cases the stick itself may sometimes become the carrot.

Sins of the Doppelgänger

by Linda Courtland

London's cobblestone streets are packed full of spirits so I wasn't all that surprised when my doppelganger turned up Tuesday night, drunk outside a pub. My ghostly double was dressed to kill, with a chic new haircut and a figure to die for. And I swear, she'd had a nose job since the last time I'd seen her. I turned my face away, ashamed of my shabby clothes and the way I'd let my body go; ghost or no ghost, there's nothing more depressing that being second best to your own damn self. The dreaded doppelganger was staggering home with a total stranger when my sweet, gentle husband walked out of the bar. He looked right through her and smiled at me, blissfully unable to ever see my dark side.

Girl in the Night

by Georgina Bruce

She wakes up in the night, and it's dark and the man next to her is snoring too loudly, shaking the black air into millions of blurry particles, and so she pushes his shoulder and he rolls away from her, leaving a cold shadow all along her thigh. They are both naked, the man and herself, and the room is chill. She gets out of bed, gropes on the floor for her t-shirt and, finding nothing, wonders how far she flung her clothing last night and whether she should pick up the man's white shirt and wear that, even though it makes her think of Hollywood movies and all the thin girls who look great in their boyfriends' shirts, with their slim thighs and smooth knees and American tans. She goes naked into the hallway and down the stairs to the kitchen, where the floor is icy underfoot, and she turns on the tap and drinks a long fresh wet pint of water, dripping splashes onto her bare chest. She goes back upstairs and into the bathroom, turning on the low humming light, and she washes her hands in the sink, and looks up to see her face in the mirror, but her reflection is not there. In the mirror is the shower curtain and the dim light, but not the girl who goes bump in the night.

Miss Broadway

by Brad Gayman

Sometimes I like to think about what other people do, the way people have personas or phrases that sum up who they are. My two favorites are Miss Broadway and Deer Hunter. Miss Broadway makes me think of glitter and sass: distaff gowns that remove to reveal dancing legs. Deer Hunter makes me think of camouflage and urine, bait and animal calls. It is interesting to think that some people know who they are, and they have places and personalities that move with them. For me, it is hard to know when to be what; it is hard to know when to be Deer Hunter and when to be Miss Broadway.

Word Bang

by Paige L. Hanson

I bought a typewriter because they said it would improve our relationship ~ props, they said, help. And no longer do writing and I meet for a post-dinner perfunctory word fuck, quickly scrawled with no spark. Oh, no. We collide at all times in a torrent of letters banged out from a daisywheel: clickety clack, clickety SMACK, baby. Mr. Jack Daniels is no longer a liquored-up third in my half-hearted slur of words stumbled on a cold computer screen. I fly on a natural high spurred by slamming keys and ribbon tape twisting and when it's over, I stretch out on top of the pages we cranked, fingers aching and inked, probably pantyless.

Why

by Lee Shafer

The manic chatter abruptly stopped as I walked into the girls' bathroom where two vaguely familiar girls' eyes darted from me to each other to the mirror in front of them before I entered a stall. "I can't believe she came to school today," one girl whispered to the other before leaving for first period. I walked through the halls of my junior high with my name falling in whispered tones around me until I reached the crowd at my defaced locker. My heart raced as my mind registered the words scrawled there *die bitch stuckup watch you back cunt* and heard her voice, "I'm going to kick your ass after school, bitch!" I barely knew the girl glaring at me with her throng of friends and barely managed the word, "Why?" The shoving, pushing, pulling, tearing and even my lip slicing open on my braces paled in comparison to never knowing why.

Impulse Buy

by Jessica Patient

On the stairs was one of Janet's open-toed, ruby red sandals that she had given her sister, after buying them from just a side glance as she dashed back to work one hectic Thursday lunchtime and finding they were only comfortable in the shop. Something wasn't right, as the shoe laid there discarded, abandoned and no one was answering to her calls. Janet had been seduced as soon as she seen the sandals in the window. Sliding her feet inside, she knew it was lust, those shoes would be dangerous. The impulse wore off as soon as she got back home, took the lid off the box and her swollen, pregnant feet could hardly fit into the shoe and she immediately marched the shoebox around to her sister so her husband didn't know about another wasteful expense. Opening the bedroom door, there in the expansive king-sized bed, her sister laid, spread out like a starfish with one leg still wearing the other ruby red shoe was on top of Janet's Husband.

Hearts, Stars, and Horseshoes

by Hailey Sowden

My relationship with my brother can be summed up by the way we eat our cereal. Whenever I buy a box of Lucky Charms he eats all the Charms and leaves just the Luckies behind. I tell him that that's not sanitary, and it's not fair; lots of cereals have Luckies, those sweetened oat puffs, Pops, Cap'n Crunch, Apple Jacks, Cheerios. The list goes on. But what our dear Irishman has is unique. It's not enough for me just to be lucky when he gets to be charmed.

An Ordinary Mary

by Tara Lazar

My life began the day my daughter died. I know most parents state the opposite, that their lives ceased to offer meaning and all that sappy shit, but I'm relieved to be free. Her father did what I dreamed about, disappearing, becoming someone else. Funny how men bitch about women's lack of composure, but shove a dying child in their face and their emotions explode like a long-dormant volcano — messy and inconvenient. I'm finally dating again, and when they ask, "Do you have any kids?" I answer as only I can. Because how can I claim to be a mother if my life began the day my daughter died?

Music Interrupted

by Nicole Andrea Aube

The French man on the CBC says listening to Messaien is like opening the door and hearing music that has already been playing forever, toujours, and will continue playing forever after the door is, once again, shut. I sit here, rapt, believing that like Messaien I am living/dying to create such an artistic phenomenon, such beauty. My obsessed, Van Gogh-yellow hands unsteadily pour more tea (I would rather, in truth, drink laudanum or starshine) while between sips my head hangs. Am I a tragic body, condemned by my own pride to make only mediocre music on the piano before me? No. I shut off the radio, set down the tea, reach for the keys, and if my ego doesn't help me eternity will.

Long Time Coming

by Elissa Cain

Late afternoon sunlight filtered through the trees and onto the sidewalk near where Dan sat quietly, his body assuming the classic pose of a man deep in thought (his posture and form were accidental for Dan wasn't a man of purposeful action, for he preferred, instead, to react); he watched absentmindedly as the rays sparkled onto the aged concrete walkway that ran parallel to a block-long expanse of Boston brownstones, the general vicinity of which was littered by random cigarette butts and a few of the first fallen leaves of the season...despite his languid position his mind was quite engaged, mulling over the concept of cutting free the loose ends of his life. Change wasn't one of his favorite occurrences in this complicated and painful dance of life, but it was the one thing he couldn't clear from his mind, despite his best efforts; after all, avoidance was one of his inherent skills and he had used it to his advantage and disadvantage repeatedly...this time, however, he would have to face the world head-on and brace himself for the impending fallout that was sure to follow. He stood up slowly, his head spinning with the choices which lay before him and turned to walk up the flight of gray stone steps that led to the front door of his apartment; just before entering, he reached over to the black iron mailbox that hung by the door and adjusted the little red flag, indicating that he had letters for the postal carrier to pick up (even though the receptacle's only inhabitants were a seven-legged spider with a homely little web that hadn't managed to capture an insect for the majority of the summer). Once in the foyer, he stopped to take a well-worn suitcase from the closet and ripped the flight tags from around the handle, then holding them between his thumb and forefinger, he rubbed the glossy paper thoughtfully as he recalled what had started out as an exciting adventure but which soon spiraled into an abyss from which there seemed no escape...not a week passed that he didn't wake up with the thought of packing his bags and moving back to his childhood home in West Virginia. Dan sighed heavily, releasing a year's worth of frustration in one drawn out breath, then walked purposefully to his bedroom, chucking the suitcase on the floor and surveying the empty leather box into which he would soon attempt to stuff the contents of his life; it seemed much smaller somehow than the last time he had opened it, and he wondered if it was possible to carry mementos of his time spent in Boston without also carrying the curse which this city had laid upon his soul. Closing his eyes for a moment as if to wipe his mental slate clean, Dan took his keys off of the night stand and walked from the bedroom to the front door, leaving the suitcase open and empty, his footsteps sounding heavy and tired on the worn and cracked wood floor; he checked his back pocket for his wallet and closed the door behind him, locking the deadbolt and shoving his hands into his pockets; the light breeze which had cooled his skin earlier was now slightly more brisk with the impending hint of autumn and Dan watched the leaves dance about under his feet as he walked, one foot in front of the other, away from his apartment and into a world filled with answerless questions; his face was blank, but a ruffle of movement began to slowly creep upon his lips until they curled into a half-cocked smile – for the first time in a long time, Dan was happy.

'67 Alien Summer

by Susan Moody

They had the proof right there in the field – a perfect circle – burned into the prairie grass where it had landed. They showed their mothers and it was dismissed as a prank. But they all told the same story - a spaceship containing little green men with pointy shoes had landed and these aliens chased them around their wooden fort on that blazing hot summer afternoon. They valiantly fought them off with rocks, sticks and clumps of dirt, hurling the objects at the little guys, who would disappear and then re-appear in another spot. This neighborhood rag-tag band of 8 and 9 year-old kids, were not only defending their fort in the field from this enemy, but their country and their honor as well, just like the war raging in Vietnam that they saw on the nightly news. So when the aliens retreated, blasting off into the summer sky and victory was finally theirs - they proudly went home – boasting of their conquest, only to be punished for lying... their story, the parent's weren't buying.

Solitary Symphony

by Eric Kramer

We scribble our final notes as the curtains rise, the still silence echoing with anticipation. In this moment we begin our masterpiece; an outpouring of words so deep and eloquent even at its most incomprehensible, a song that grows more beautiful than even the grandest of orchestras could play. This is our opera, our concerto, woven seamlessly by the rawest, purest emotions. Our expressions accompanied with crescendo and diminuendo, scored at lengths of quarters and halves, rests and dotted eighths. Our voices fall to the quietest of pianos, then rise to the most grandiose of fortissimo that could shake the largest of concert halls to its very core. And as the symphony comes to its climax, as it ends with uproarious applause, the world will see it is a work that not even God himself could triumph.

Part 2

Too Much to Lose

by Juliana Perry

Sitting on the couch the other night, wondering what a 35-year-old should be doing, she moved her arm up and with closed fingers which rounded her breast and palpated in small circles. The moment was random and not planned, but instead as impulsive as most moments are for her. Knowing what a woman knows about her anatomy, knowing what the physicians tell them, knowing beyond this because the big C runs in the family; palpitating around gently, across something. Wait, back again across, not smooth, not there in that one place. Again, one more time, because she suddenly has a knot in her stomach and wants her own mother while she begins getting the children into pajamas. The lump in her throat matches the other one in her breast as she comforts each child and lays them down to sleep for the night.

Shelbyville, Indiana

by Steve Talbert

Shelbyville, Indiana, isn't "Tinsel Town" or "Sin City," but there is plenty to see and do if you know where to look. Home to the late Edna Parker, the former "Oldest Living Woman," and Sandy Allen, the former "World's Tallest Woman," Shelbyville has hosted countless celebrities, including former presidents Bill Clinton and the late Ronald Reagan, the late Ricky Nelson, the Oakridge Boys, Kenny Loggins, Jerry Reed, the late Sam Walton, the Guess Who, Three Dog Night and many others. We've got Denny's, KFC, Taco Bell, Burger King, two Wendy's, four McDonald's, and we're scheduled to get a White Castle in 2010. Our historic downtown features a quaint, independently owned bookstore and a prank shops that sells Halloween costumes in the front and adult items in the back. We are one of few American cities that can boast both a drive-in movie theatre and a casino. So, if you're ever in Central Indiana, swing by Shelbyville for a look-see, enjoy a breaded tenderloin at the Cow Palace and have someone snap your picture in front of the statue of a man holding two bear cubs.

Father

by Doug McIntire

Though I didn't want to be there, I knew it wasn't a choice as I followed my brother through the heavy set of double doors, my senses immediately assaulted by the overpowering stench of piss and things worse. We traversed the maze of sterile halls as he led me unerringly to our father's room. And although warned of what to expect, I was shocked when I saw him, as words alone could not adequately convey the gravity of his condition. The giant oak-tree-of-a-man whom I had once deemed immutable lay before me, a skeleton with skin, unconscious and bare, save a skewed blanket that did little to respect what might have remained of his dignity. His tormented dreams and tortured moans made it unclear whether he was fighting for life or painfully awaiting death. I could only sit with him and pretend that my presence somehow comforted him, but I knew it was a façade; the part of him who had once been my father was already gone.

They Shimmer

by Jodi MacArthur

They shimmer, the jewels that lie buried under the sand. Little suns of Babylon, they were called in times past, when the living revered the dead, and when the dead fancied the living. They will rise again soon, cloaked by evening's purple hues, crowned by purest golden stars. Souls denied, stolen, branded in sculptures of rock while vultures ever circle, keeping watch. Yes, they will rise seeking those that follow after the razor cut edges of modern design, sharp angles of modern belief. And then what will we do, and then what will we do?

Stay With Me Then

by Keturah Jones

The night is not yet so dark that I can't see your face. The wind is not yet so strong that I can't hear your voice. For in this place of bombs and sirens I still know your love. And in this world of terror you still walk me safely home. So when the stars fall from the sky, the moon turns red and the earth turns dry, stay with me then. And teach me how to hope, to trust, to stand, when my mountains of certainty crumble into shifting sand.

The Graveyard Girl

by Alyssa Ning

She is the living among the dead, the guardian angel of the departed. The sight of her, wandering the burial grounds at night, with her porcelain skin and long flowing hair, always gave me a sense of placidity. I imagine she smells like the flowers she brings for the dead, a mix of carnation, daffodil, sunflower, and lily of the valley, always freshly plucked, always beautifully arranged. No one is quite sure of her identity – whether she is lamenting the loss of a young love or the death of her grandmother, whether she is an orphan, the dutiful daughter visiting her parents or an inspired student, paying her respect to a beloved mentor. I believe she is none of those and all of those. I believe she is the nightingale of the dead, the keeper of spirit.

Seeing in Darkness

by Natalie Jabbar

The mysterious forces like to visit her at night. They creep into her slumber like hooded men, shouldering satchels of premonitions that they empty into her dreams. Series of initials, hazy images, faces without names, names without faces. These are the kinds of dreams you beg to be woken up from. When such nights transpire, she wakes up looking different. It is as if a part of her has been sacrificed for the visions.

Los Perros de Belice

by Diane Brady

They are everywhere – in the cities, towns and smallest villages – half-starved mongrels with vacant eyes, roaming the streets by day and night, darting out to chase my bicycle, snarling with teeth bared, growling, barking. When I walk and feel threatened, I lean over to grab a stone from the street, and before my hand reaches it, the menacing canines turn on cue and wander away. The dogs with homes are often abused and fed table scraps – chicken bones, rice, beans, tortillas; the strays are masters of survival, aggressive in their quest for food, pillaging yards for the garbage often left to rot in heaping piles; the females bear litter after litter, their bellies overstretched and hanging, the puppies sickly. I have owned several dogs during my life and years ago treated a beloved Alaskan Husky diagnosed with Diabetes for nearly two years, giving him insulin injections every 12 hours; I love dogs; I love all animals big and small. But in this developing country, the greatest cultural difference I will never truly accept is the role of the dog; for in Belize dogs are guardians of the property, bred to attack and bite anyone who invades their territory; they are not pets. And so it was one day as I walked side-by-side with my landlord through her backyard to the gate between our two properties, the dog untied but sitting quietly beside it's owner's house; five feet from our destination it rushed up from behind in a sneak attack, first grabbing my right calf to stop my gait and then clamping it's massive jaws around the front of my leg ~ the horror of seeing the dog's head attached to me, the landlord's blow to release it's grip, the blood and raw tissue dangling; after the rabies shots, the antibiotics, the bandaging, I am still healing – although the front of my leg remains numb; but it is my spirit that is the most damaged – for as a dog lover, Los Perros de Belice will leave a scar in my heart far deeper than the one I visibly bear.

The Parameters of Love

by Sondra Sula

Is it possible to be in love with a wheel of cheese? Even if it is brie, laced in raspberry jam, and scattered with walnuts? Would someone whittle away at their lover with a knife? Perhaps. Indeed. Oh, Brie, come rest upon my pink tongue, visit my lonely molars, dive down my cavernous throat and find your way into my eager, empty stomach.

Water Buffalo

by Steve Edgehouse

After our neighborhood flooded in 1990, and our septic tanks seeped into our water wells, FEMA sent us an Army-issued M149 water buffalo, a 400 gallon, camouflaged trailer we could get fresh water from for bathing, drinking, cooking and cleaning. I was fourteen and, with Dad working as much overtime at the coal mine as possible so we could move to a less flood-able town ASAP, I was more or less the man of the (muddy, stinky, warped-floor) house, which is a nice way of saying I had to carry gallon milk jugs, four at a time, to the buffalo to retrieve water whenever anybody in my extended family needed any. On a day like any other that summer--humid and sticky, Clorox in the air, everybody's living room furniture on tarps in their front yards--I was lugging my jugs to the buffalo, and once it was in sight I saw the Action 11 News Team there, setting up a live remote for the six o'clock news. I've never been the sort to have my picture taken for Christmas cards, much less be on the news, so I turned around and walked home and told my mom and little brother Troy what was happening. Troy, to his photogenic credit, never met a camera he didn't like; he put on his "dress" Cleveland Indians hat, grabbed two jugs out of my hand, and out the door he went for his first (and, as time would prove, only) trip. Action 11 filmed him walking to the buffalo, working the spigot, filling the jugs, talking about how tedious the water-fetching process was for everybody in town, and we taped the news that night, and Troy will happily bust that tape out if the mood is right and you've got a VCR.

Darl'n

by Timothy P. Remp

"Just you and me now," Abraham said, stroking his mustache as Holland left the card table and out the swinging door. All Connor had left was the deed to the saloon and his share from the last stagecoach robbery, stashed in a cigar box under a floorboard behind the bar ~ but no one, not even his mistress, Miss Sally, knew of it. "Darl'n', just bring me the bottle," Abraham said to Miss Sally with a wink. Miss Sally swaggered from behind the bar holding a half empty whiskey bottle, approached the table and swung the bottle hard against the back of Connor's head, glass shards and bloody cards ending the game. "Good for noth'n," Miss Sally spat as she kicked Connor's body to the floor. With a laugh and a wink, she leaned over the table and purred, "Cigar, Darl'n?"

A Note to Mr. Smith

by Emily Sheer

"Dinner may be late tonight," she wrote, in haste with blue pen, "I've got things to do like: grocery shop, weed my garden, exchange recipes, learn fluent French, leave this town, assimilate into my new foreign surroundings and live a happy life." She took in a few deep breaths. She could do this. She could do this! Crossing everything out she simply wrote, "Leaving here seems to be such a hassle." She pulled the trigger and fell onto the hard, cold linoleum; she was all alone.

Don't Look Down

by Pamila Payne

We'd been sunbathing in the back yard, lolling on towels in the grass, Sue turning her usual blushed bronze, me, my usual scorched milk. Sue rolled over onto her back, shielded her eyes with her hand and looked up at the tree in the back corner of the yard, its summer leaves still lush and lively despite the heat. She said, "God, I used to love to climb trees..." and the next thing I knew, we were as high up as we could get in it, surveying the yard in shady secrecy, whispering about all the things we never talked about: my mom, her man, the pounds of PCP hidden in the garage, layering its ugly pall of menthol jet fuel all over everything. We heard the growl of him coming up the street and knew how it was from the needless revving of his Dirty Mary Charger as it roared up into the front yard. The hollering started up as soon as he slammed the front door, "SUE!" stomped through the house, "SUE!" threw open the back door, "SUE!" barreled out into the yard to kick furiously at our abandoned towels and cast his seeking glare in every direction. We sat lightly on our branches, still-breath bathing beauties, staring into each others eyes to keep from looking down at the man below, who would surely sense the gaze of prey and look up.

Boise Butcher

by Doug Mathewson

I knew a girl for a while whose dad was a butcher, working different chain grocery stores around Boise over the years. He drank real hard and regular, whether this made him restless or his restless ways kept him drinking, I don't know. He moved from job to job as time went on, as he and his knives wore down. I thought then that a drunk with a cleaver was bad medicine for sure. The girl moved on too, restless like her dad, so I never made the seven hour trip to Boise to meet her folks. Somebody said she works for the phone company, but I don't know that for sure.

Madness in Motion

by Chris Roberts

And I am supreme madness. And every schizophrenic association of the cognitive mind. And every outburst of flame in the words of a schizophrenic and every grandiose height of soprano song of this beautifully wracking affliction. And I am bi-polar. And the impossible heightened sensation of being alive and the non-stop imagination and the insane rush of rapid thoughts and action. And I am the empty shell of feelings and the desperate candle that flickers low and in constant danger of the fatal wind of suicide that in its joy howls relentless forever and ever.

Resolutions

by Paige Turner

This year: I'm going to take my coffee black. I'm going to remember the way your head looked on my pillow when I wake up alone. I'm going to fit the pieces of my heart back together while some of your love is still inside of it. I'm going to floss twice a day. I'm going to smile at my demons. And every time I kiss I'll remember to open my heart and close my eyes.

Through Her They Die

by Shelly Rae Rich

The mountain was harsh and cruel all through the winter, but when he looked at her, into those eyes, he felt the push of young buds, the pitch of the oceans, the flutter of cool tender leaves in invisible sheets of mist. Noel called out just to hear the sound of Anisette's voice. Her kiss was sex, her sex coupling, her hand one pair. In the mornings, Noel held tightly as Anisette soared, sparkling glints flashing like flecks of gold in a rushing stream, and though she was removed from him in those hours, there was no room for temporary loss or sorrow, no. It was replaced with fire of sainthood, the earth below him, the breeze that carried, the water that cleansed, and those plus forces of passion, elegiac went as well. There were rumors and whispers, but the secret was everything and no more than the fact that her eyes were green.

Skinny Dipping

by Salvatore Buttaci

We called him "Skinny" for the same reason his slow-witted brother Tommy was "Einstein." Skinny weighed over 200 pounds, and we were only in the fifth grade! Oddly enough he played dynamite basketball where we met Thursday nights in the basement gym of St. Clare's Church. "Boys," said Father Paddy Conway before last week's game, "I have a wee problem: someone's been raiding the poor box upstairs." At the break, Skinny took off and I followed him into the dark church where I saw Skinny dipping his fat hand into the poor box. When he heard me call out his name, he turned and called back over his shoulder, "I'm puttin' it back 'cause, hey, I ain't no thief!"

Travel Guide

by Donna Kirk

I am sitting on the roof of a brick Victorian next a guy I just met with our backs pressed against a large white cupola that is six feet high with a pointed copper dome and a metal rooster spinning like crazy on top. He says he's a journalist who lives in DC two blocks from here -- where we bumped into each other, literally -- and after he helped me pick up the stack of books I was carrying, we ended up walking twelve blocks together talking about our favorite writers, dropped my books off at the library, had an impromptu lunch and then for some reason I followed him here after climbing a black ladder on the side of this municipal building because he assured me that "the view of the whole city is fantastic." So, while I nervously smoke his cigarettes and look in confusion at a view of a loading dock, he begins to tell me about his travels: the hoodoos and orange rocks in Utah, the tiny fragile cups of chocolate in Milan, the farmer in Switzerland who climbed down a terrifying ridge to save an old heffer while singing a German hymn only to vanish and how the tropical bodies of Miami lounge on white sand bronzed and beautiful. It sounds great but now I am terrified because it is dusk in Washington DC, I am with a stranger who claims that this precipice with a view of packing material is his favorite place in the world to write travel articles and sitting at a sharp slant in the gusting wind holding on to the peak of a roof is the most dangerous thing I have ever done in ~ what would now appear to be ~ my painfully ordinary life. But, when he finally pulls back a faded green shudder on the side of the cupola I see a hectagonal room inside with a tall ceiling and enough space to sit comfortably with my legs out in front of me while all around the room there is a white sill like a continuous shelf upon which someone has neatly organized some things: a yellowed book of Marquez; a smudged pamphlet of world maps; blue pens; a big black journal bound with twine and stuffed with clippings, post-cards, photos, maps and his published articles; a beeswax candle; a pair of binoculars and a sleeping bag rolled up and leaning against the wall. I'm stunned when he props open a shudder on the other side because suddenly there is the entire city smug in the after-glow of a gorgeous sunset.

Footprints

by Peggy McFarland

For the past ten years, he swept away the muddy footprints that led from the lake's edge onto the porch, continued into the house, up the stairwell and tracked to the foot of his bed. He removed the carpet after the first year. Her nocturnal visits left a stagnant sogginess and a lingering, decomposing reek... better to keep the floor bare. That first year was hardest, a nightmarish blur of eyes bulging as her lids decomposed; fingernails lengthening into blackened claws; clumped hair exposing milky bone; bloated, discolored skin molting off until a grinning skull and bare skeleton commanded his attention. But now, anticipation replaced dread as he watched her skeletal remains slowly regain human form, metamorphosing into her youthful self and then emanating light and hope as his own corporal form succumbed to the disease that rotted his insides the way the lake had rotted her. At nightfall, he would meet her at lake's edge, accept her hand and for better or worse, let her lead him to forever.

The Moment She Relented

by Kelley A. Swan

She clutched her son to her chest and laid her hand protectively across his skull, warding off the doctor's ridiculous words. While the surgeon spoke, she sat and stared and memorized every wrinkle, freckle, and line of his hands-the ones that would mutilate her son, that would fix her son. But, again, he said those words, cranial birth defect and "Sagittal Synostosis," and she found herself wondering who conjured such stupid names for these things or what good the diplomas lining his office were (mere slips of papers set in glass and wood), or just what kind of man enjoyed cutting into human flesh, even if to heal. "I know Christmas is only next week, but I'd like to schedule surgery right way." Anger flooded her then, making her want to lunge across his desk and scatter the notes and pencils and pictures and frames cluttering its surface and fling them so they hit the walls and they struck the floor and to wrap her hands around the skinny chicken neck of this man who wanted to cut into her baby, hurt her baby, in order to help her baby, and just choke the living crap out of him. But instead, she stared once more at the doctor as he smiled at her kindly, at his bald head and the way his eyes crinkled behind his glasses and how he looked so much like Frank Perdue, and relented by saying, "Yes, please, thank you," because, really, what else could she do?

Beaching Dragons

by Absolutely*Kate

From a private distance I watched the lone woman in the sway of the purple skirt and moss green yet-a-summer shirt stride her glide across the Septembered sands of Jones Beach, drawn by either inner demons or concentric majestic magnetic forces beyond mere human capacities to cooly comprehend. Right into the raw crash of churning surf rising, rising did the purpose of her purposeful stride collide... as I experienced her experience of primal need to gather soul from swirl in what Madre Nature could supremely splash-provide. At one with all the powers and secrets of the sea was she, fully clothed and fully aware of the vast pullings which had pulled her there... time traveling as the hour glass of sands give up their true grit. He watched too, that dark bearded beach man with his eyes soft and his heart's grin wide*open large and his arms outstretched to catch her walk-into embrace that suspended time and place while waves ran cross current around them... fully knowing this time was their one and only time, apparitions of soul*mating morphed real to face the daunt past taunt which the twenty-five radiation zaps would mean to her conquering as they began their burning beguine the very next morrow. Two wrong-place, wrong-time great souls across time, thus the more strengthened from this day's tempestuous rampage of la mer and l'amour, gave kisses rather than words more poignantly... right there on their shore. The simple strength of the shiny silver cd her DJ*man pressed into her palm upon their parting expresses part of her still... for I am that lone woman, now so much a part of so many... who slayed the dragon of cancer's damnation, while Harry Nilsson plays on - "As Time Goes By" and his revered schmaltzy rendition of "Remember," for my memories too survive, 'cross that beach, 'cross that time.

Down to Earth

by Diane Becker

He ran his forefinger round the rim of the lid then sucked at his fingertip. The texture's like chalk, he thought, it tastes of earth. He hadn't anticipated this – but dipped his finger in again and swallowed. It was like scraping your tongue against a blackboard on which someone had scrawled every equation ever written. A perfect solution, he thought, as he licked his lips and wiped specks of dust from the corners of his mouth. Finally he screwed the lid back on and reaching up to the highest shelf, wedged the urn in between his favorite books.

The Tigress Moment

by Maggie Whitehead

We were talking about the most influential thing someone had ever said to us - you know, the thing that made us change our life's direction, or gave our life direction, or some other such bullshit. I never did share mine, but it was easy enough to recall: it was the moment when Bill McIntire, sitting next to me in the cafeteria of Plymouth High School, told me that I struck him as "the sort of girl who gets beaten." It was a spectacularly ignorant thing to say, however Bill was generally a good guy, so rather than being malicious what I think he was probably trying (but failing) to say was that he worried about me - that he perceived me as impressionable, delicate and easily victimized, and he genuinely thought this was something I needed to know. What bothered me most wasn't that he said it, but that he was sort of right, and deep down I sort of knew it. And that's the moment that changed everything - the moment when I stopped worrying about harmony, the moment when "sure" ceased to be a rote response to all requests, the moment I stopped trying so hard to be liked, and the moment I stopped aiming to please. In short, it was the moment I became a tigress - unafraid to growl, unashamed to claw, and not really giving a good goddamn if that scares the little boys.

Absolution

by Rayne Debski

His two-year-old granddaughter sits on his lap and pulls at his ear, laughing at his protests, unaware of the pain she inflicts. In her touch he feels the vulnerability of childhood; in her navy eyes, he sees her appraisal of him: she can get away with anything. When she tugs harder, he takes her soft hand with its pale fingernails and places it against his face, holds it there and remembers the softness of another child, a previous edition of this one, the daughter who roiled his blood with her carelessness, and got away with nothing but memories of a bad-tempered father. Years later he can still recall the sensation of his hand striking her, the disbelief on her face, and the shame he couldn't avoid. That daughter, with the wariness of adulthood, watches him hold her child. The toddler pulls hard enough on his ear to make him frown; the mother reaches for her child, but he refuses to release her, instead ruffles the girl's hair with a forgiving kiss, believing the startled look crossing his daughter's face is remembrance, and the smile she finally gives him is absolution.

Bacon

by Heather Leet

The worst smell I have ever known floated on the breeze while we waited for the school bus at the end of our driveway every spring as the pigs were slaughtered on the Pendleton farm. They burn the hair off the hogs prior to slaughter and that mixed with the coppery smell of blood is nauseating. We would cover our faces with our tee shirts trying to keep the smell at bay. My sister and brother have wiped the memory from their minds, but I remember every detail of every spring from the age of seven to seventeen. I think what made the smell so bad was the fear you could hear in their squealing as they took their last breaths. Surprisingly, I still love the taste of bacon.

Hey, I'm a 6!

by Daniel Stine

A numerologist approached me electronically selling saccharine sagaciousness, telling me I was a number 6 and he had something he had to get off his chest about my imminent future. First he tickled me with tantalizing tidbits of who I am and my place in the grand scheme of all things numerological and how by understanding my "6-ness" I could better influence my destiny, enhance it even. Then he educated me with erudite readings on the four cores of numerology, the Life Path Number, the Expression Number, Soul Urge Number, and the Destiny Number, using caps to underscore the importance of these, the four core. He goes on to play a shell game with the numbers, the Number 9 is your adversary and the Number 3 is your best mate and numerically speaking you should generally avoid all other Number 6's. He confidently confided in me that the Number 6 was a very charitable number as he counted out the many traits I as a 6 possess; traits such as The Protector, Provider, Healer, Nurturing, Children, Empathy, Intuition, Sympathy, Quality, Sustenance, Love of Community, Unconditional love, Circulation, Economy, Agriculture, Balance, Grace, Evolution, Simplicity, and Sorcery. And then, once I was numerically entranced, he threw another batch of numbers my way, numbers with dollar signs and discounts, and buy 1 get 9 free, and he gave me a number in date format saying this is the best date for this particular transaction as it affects my entire destiny and please send me your numbers as in bank account numbers and I responded by deleting a number of emails.

Point of Departure

by Tovli Simiryan

Gerda decided footprints left behind were like pieces of silence drenched with an accelerant looking for a flame with wings. When she was twelve, an unusual imprint on a mound of sand so intrigued her, she scooped the moist earth into the palm of her hand, deposited it inside a tiny yellow scarf and slid it into her coat pocket. Once a year, on her birthday, she unfolded the indentation she'd captured from its cloth home and remembered her past. The day her ninety-ninth year began, Gerda opened the scarf and discovered her footprint had dried into an unrecognizable turmoil of mismatched slivers of stone and grains of dark sand. The next day, while walking in her garden, she attempted to free what remained inside her pockets, lost her balance, fell and died the instant the yellow scarf released its secrets. Shards of rock and miniscule portions of earth, unseen for nearly a century, flew like smoke into a spring day and rained on tender leaves with such an odd glitter, little birds learning to fly were frightened and ignited into song.

Night Creatures Union 763

by Thom Gabrukiewicz

Of course they gathered at night, the fairies, pixies, the imps, your assorted goblins, trolls and Korrigans, beneath an arena of wild nightshade that grabbed at trees with sticky vines. Ever since they voted to unionize, these meetings had grown fractured, tedious. There were the diminutive and delicate fairies, who always pushed for more entitlements to the children who ventured into the forest; more, more more, always granting, never taking - opposite of the trolls and goblins, who voted in a block, and as always wished simply to eat the young interlopers. Just getting the pixies to sit - quietly - stretched Roberts Rules of Order to breaking; at their worst, they'd shower the imps with sparkling dust in a kaleidoscope of colors and then cackle in tiny voices that sounded like the constant crinkle of crushed Christmas paper. Then there were the Korrigans, who sat in the back on a rotted stump, jaded, and mumbled all-encompassing insults in-between spitting sunflower hulls into their stunted hands, their wrinkled palms. Control, console and cajole the Korrigans, the fairies knew, and their agenda would win.

Space Invaders

by Doug Mathewson

Space invaders from above, so horrifying to behold, wave upon wave of missile-proof metal ships descending form the sky! With terrifying visage they march upon our fair metropolis, mornings light discarded in refraction by gleaming amour-plated suits. Cruel tridents ring with each lock-step strike upon ground to mark the measure of their advancing cadence, as with steely swords raised aloft in unison they chant and march as one. Shrill clockwork voice boxes proclaim with flat delivery our inevitable demise in crude inhuman clicking imitation of our earthly mother tongue. The situation was desperate, and looked bleak for all mankind till New Jersey Teamsters did arise from Newark's scrap-yard bowels, striking back with harshest vengeance and monstrous grapple cranes cutting wide swaths with huge magnetic booms. We weep with joy and laughter now, and our hearts delight as China bound by cargo ship this formerly fierce army goes, crushed and bailed, sold by weight to embrace a new and unanticipated destiny beneath the stars, newly minted as products made by Kitchen-Aid.

FM Noise

by Rod Drake

It was dark when I got home; the radio we always leave on to make thieves think someone is there was blasting loud, harsh, popping static. I turned the radio off quickly, and it became perfectly quiet in my cold, empty apartment. I wondered how this could have happened; the radio was on the regular station with its strong, clear signal when I left this morning. My ex-girlfriend and roommate Veronica must have tuned it to this horrible sound for spite - she still has her key to the apartment. And a grudge it would seem. Even so, I miss her.

Dance Macabre

by Nathalie Boisard-Beudin

In and out of the storm did the dunes dance, snaking along invisible boundaries of reality while the sorcerer held his staff high, stirring the elements. No music but the hiss of century trimmed pebbles stroking against their sort; no music but the howl of winds above and yet they danced. Grain after grain, landslide after landslide, the sinuous ballet progressed, the whirls and twirls eating nature around them, smothering life under a russet dust coffin. When the dunes finally reached their goal – swallowing it in one lazy yet ineluctable move - and the last plant had disappeared in their golden maws, only then did the sorcerer let them rest, lowering his wand, placating winds inside his ample coat, bringing the world into a standstill so he could admire his creation: Sand - oceans of sand as far as the eye could reach and beyond – all life erased from earth but his own. Soon he would disappear too and then the planet would finally be left alone, free to find yet another equilibrium so it could start again the process of life, unhindered by the murderous, polluting, influence of mankind this time. And he saw that this was good.

The Art of Being Observant

by Christine Taylor

Carrie's eyes shot open on a sudden realization that the annoying music in her dream was, in fact, coming from the cell phone alarm on her bedside table; and that she had drowsily endured it for a very, very long time. She flung out of warm covers into a cold bedroom, starting in with her daily why-am-I-always-late-litany as she grabbed random articles of clothing and made tracks for the bathroom, ruefully aware that a shower would be the only comfort she'd get that day, since breakfast obviously wasn't going to make the cut. Ten minutes and a slug of instant decaf coffee later--decaf only because she'd grabbed the wrong jar--she dawned upon the outside world, shocked at the heavy fog that enveloped the coastal neighborhood...and immediately regretful of her light blouse and cardigan, which proved to be very poor wardrobe selections indeed. While her mental litany took on a tune of "should have gone to bed earlier," her car sped through highway traffic and off to a eucalyptus-bordered side road, deserted except for the mist-shrouded silhouette of a limping jogger, who--Carrie thought just before she forgot him and pulled into the college campus--was probably a happier soul than she, as he most likely had a hot breakfast ahead of him. She parked and jumped out of her car, shivering at the cold hands of fog that pressed against her back, made her blouse stick unpleasantly to her skin; shivered again when she took a shortcut past the new construction area and narrowly avoided gashing herself on a loose fence wire, which was thigh-high--just the right height for hurrying, unsuspecting students to fall afoul of, she thought bitterly and briefly as the quad came into view. The courtyard was crowded, packed with jabbering people, people she tried to dodge while she ran, glancing at her watch, half-hearing scraps of words like "police," "murdered," "manhunt," and "construction"--words that made her cringe with inner cold as well as outer, made the door of her classroom look all the more inviting, as she pulled it open with relief and collapsed in a seat, squinting to focus on the chalkboard and its heading: "Private Investigation - Lesson Three: The Art of Being Observant."

He Says, She Says

by Jasmin Guleria

You say you miss me. I raise my eyebrows in speculation while I think to myself, "2 weeks, 2 meetings, and you miss me?" You miss my skin, my lips, the arching back and tangled web of arms and legs in rumpled sheets. You say you miss me and i laugh. Artificial laughter fills the room as you grin sheepishly. You're worried that I see right through you; I lean in and kiss you deeply, hoping my mouth will assure you that I missed you too and wondering if you see right through me.

Time to Kill

by Keturah Jones

Strathfield Station had always been a hub of activity where people arrived and departed, pushed and pulled along by ramps going up onto platforms and down into its dark cavern. Serious suits shuffled up ramps for trains to the city and school uniforms milled around in groups downstairs, ushered along by stern faced teachers at eight am. The florist and the news stand attracted their usual customers, the station master checked tickets and lovers stood kissing in corners; everyone inhaled the aroma of biscuits baking that drifted along the tracks from the factory up the line. This happened every day, except for the day when there were no suits or uniforms and the station seemed quiet, even for a weekend. Some mad man with a rifle in a postal tube left the station that morning and roamed through Strathfield Mall firing random shots into a coffee shop. I always thought the sign above the ramp leading down from Platform Three was problematic: ***Do you have time to kill? Go shopping at Strathfield Mall.***

Part 3

Driver's Ed

by Hailey Sowden

Why am I getting a bus pass? Well, when I stop at stop signs I look to my left, to my right, to the left once more, press my foot to the gas, inch forward, but this truck, this gargantuan truck comes out of nowhere, t-bones us, crushes my little car like the fist of God. My head gets stuck, pinned with my left cheek hugging the wheel, so that all I can see is my mother in the passenger seat, netted with diamond shards of the shattered window. Each bead of glass finds itself a bead of blood and by some strange alchemy becomes a sequin- a red sequin. These sequins, they cover her, frame her face, scale her legs, she becomes a glamorous showgirl dying a famous death and with my head stuck all I can do is watch. It's the same everyday at every stop sign and that's why I'm buying a bus pass.

Rapture

by Ben Spivey

Heaven opened and my father began to sing. Raising violin noise and deep piano bursts. Transcendent harmony turned into the sound of crying children. Things uprooted from earth and flew towards the vibrating song in the sky. I will keep you, I will keep you, I will keep you, was in my bones, in my mouth. All around me.

Workplace Bathroom Confessions

by Ryan W. Bradley

When I piss at work I leave the bathroom door open so I can hear if customers come into the store. Sometimes I hear the bells on the door and know people have come in, but I can't stop myself midstream, and I know they can probably hear me. The red curtain between the store and the back room isn't soundproof, after all. Sometimes I imagine my wife coming in the store and hearing me, and pretending she's not my wife she stalks into the back room and peers into the bathroom at me. I have my left hand cupped underneath my testicles and she says something in a soft voice, maybe "nice form" or "need a hand?" Maybe one out of five times I forget to zip my jeans back up, I don't know where my head gets to, but it's good that my wife already married me before I sent this email to her.

Not Today

by Tess Dickenson

How she wished that just once... just one random day... she could have polished the golden wood floors to a level of perfection that would earn approval. She loved those floors... the magic that could be wielded with a floor buffer... wiping away the imperfections of another day... leaving behind a gleaming surface. Some days she would imagine the scuffs to be the miseries of her heart, relishing the moment of make-believe control as the brushes whisked them away Then there were the hours of patrolling the entrances to the room, guarding against little footprints... daring dust to settle... protecting the perfection... waiting in anticipation for the eyes of the one who mattered most. At last the car pulls into the driveway... a dog barks... a key rattles in the door... and he steps into the house ornamented with the aroma of pot roast and baking rolls. "Oh... you didn't get to the floors today?"

Perspective

by Sherrie Pilkington

He reached for the sky; I reached for the metal rail wishing it were a safety bar across my lap. His hands were open, fingers relaxed; my fingernails dug into the flesh of my palms producing knuckles that could glow in the dark. The clackity-clack stopped as the car crested the knoll; mechanics inched us forward, then momentum took over. My son's voice was pure excitement; mine reached heaven in a murderous decibel. As I exited the ride, light headed and palms wringing wet, the attendant stepped in front of me. "Lady, we permit parents to ride with their children as a courtesy, you however are scaring the little ones and that is one thing we don't permit here in Kiddie Land."

Not So Fiery

by Oceana Setaysha

Outside, it's raining like the world is ending, so I jump on my bike and ride to meet an apocalypse. Raindrops fall and crash on me like old hopes and dreams, not quite forgotten, yet too fused in the past to be held. They glance off me ever faster now as I glide, skidding over flooded footpaths, but I don't look back to see them swallowed by eternity. I reach the cliffs and look out over the ocean, barely seeing the boats I dream of escaping on, to the seas where I belong. The water, like the future, is clouded as the rain falls ever harder. Lightning strikes and I flinch, peddling my cowardly horse to its stable, not yet ready to meet the apocalypse at hand.

Money Shot

by Donna Martines

I'm waiting patiently... camera at the ready, zoom adjusted, focus set, finger poised over the shutter button... this vantage point is superb. I'm standing a few feet from where he'll play, breathlessly anticipating his entrance. Not surprisingly, I'm channeling the memories of a love struck thirteen year old covered in band buttons with her big perm held in place by Aquanet... studying him as he lingers to one side, adjusting the strings of his bass while tossing coy glances to the house. The band is tuning up, signaling an imminent start, as he paces waiting for his cue... fidgeting with his earpiece during the cacophony created by an ocean of hysterical admirers. Cherry ice cream, smile... enraptured, besotted. I'm so close I can see the wax on his strings. Syncopation.

On the Game

by Valerie O'Riordan

I thought speed dating would be a little like one of these Sixes - neat and concise and kind of satisfying - so I wrote out a list of interesting facts about myself and then spent ages paring it down to the essentials. I ended up with a bullet-point document that portrayed me in a kind of elemental, pure way, like a perfume or a haiku or a really, really, short resume. I had a few copies made up and laminated, and I stashed them at my parents' house and in my office, just in case they'd come in handy, and anyway I reckoned I could always use them as bookmarks, and then when I opened the book, I'd get a little on-the-spot confidence booster - genius. Anyway, on my way to the speed-dating event, I take a quick detour to stick one through my ex-girlfriend's letterbox, just to remind her what a loser she is, and I'm standing on the driveway polishing the card with my sleeve when a cop-car pulls up. The cop comes strutting over, takes one long look at me in my dress-to-impress leather-and-lace speed-date outfit, inspects my calling card, spits on it, spits on me, cuffs me up and hauls me in and charges me with soliciting. Concise and satisfying, my ass.

If the Shoe Fits

by Tammi J. Truax

I'm not particularly proud of it, but neither am I ashamed. I too, have thrown a shoe at a man's head. I can attest that it is a desperate act of protest, anguish, and enunciation committed by an individual who has tried to communicate in more rationale means, but has gone unheard, or worse yet, been dismissed. Fortunately for the dismisser (or decider) the only piece we are packing is a penny loafer. Perhaps, deep down, we don't really want to take out the aimed at enemy, but only to knock his ignoble crown askew. To volley back with a cocky grin really just invites the other shoe, which might just be a stealthy stilletto.

Clocked

by Steve Edgehouse

I had a student in my freshman comp class last semester, DJ, who was the starting left tackle for the football team, who was about six-six two-sixty, who usually wrote about reality television, and who was habitually fifteen minutes late to class. I'd let his lateness slide because he could be counted on to make meaningful contributions to class discussions once he lumbered from the door to his front-row seat by the window, but after about a half dozen tardies, enough was enough. The first class after spring break DJ was late, so as I was taking roll, I warned the rest of class that I was going to yell at him from the time he walked in the door until the time he took his seat, hoping that such a walk of shame might make him more punctual. Specifically, I told them I was going to ask DJ what time it was and what time class started, over and over until he was seated and ready to learn. When the door to the classroom opened, I turned from the chalkboard, and in my deepest teacher intonation, I asked DJ what time it was, and hand to God, he was wearing a gigantic Flava Flav Afrocentric clock around his neck. Everybody laughed and he was never late again.

Love

by Tracy Shields

We always do it missionary; you above me, staring down. Me, buried in the tattoos on your right arm. Buried between the pin-up and the Devil with a cigarette, the eight ball at my nose, the dice at my eyes. Silently, you ask me to tuck away my need for something deeper and save it for another time. Yet somewhere in between the vulgar emptiness and tired release, you always say, "I love you." As if you knew that seeing God were not enough.

Returning

by Susan Moody

Home for me is still the split level on Prairie Avenue , where if blindfolded, I could make my way around the interior, all the while narrating details of each and everything I touch and breathe in. The same home where my parents raised eight children, having only three bedrooms, one bathroom and we never, ever felt crowded, just blessed. With its well-worn wooden stairs, the middle of each tread pounded smooth by a million plus footsteps over all these years. Its long expanse of a backyard where the grass eventually turns into stone and flows up against the late-night-rumbling-freight tracks. I have adapted to changes of location with the ebb and flow of life, but it still doesn't sit well within me. I am so thankful that my Momma still lives in that house, for I always know when things get hectic and I need some inner rebalancing, where I can run – 651.

In the Dog House

by Paul D. Brazill

Bonny is so angry that she can hardly speak but, unfortunately for me, hardly is the operative word here and, as she tries to scrub the blood from my best white shirt, she goes on and on about the meal she'd cooked the night before, how long it had taken her to cook it, asking me if I wanted to live on burgers all my life and why, if I was going to spend all of my time hanging around a warehouse with a bunch of losers that look like Blues Brothers rejects, I couldn't at least call to say I won't be home. My head is hurting and my stomach is rumbling and Bonny is starting to sound like a duck, quack quack quacking, so I turn on the radio hoping it isn't more 'Sounds of the Seventies,' as I've really had my fill of that shit the last few days. The DJ's monotone drone introduces some LA band destroying a Neil Diamond classic and I switch it off, noticing that the heat from Bonny's volcano has started to cool down and I present her with a bag containing the proceeds of my recent job. When she sees the coins in the bag Bonny's jaw drops so much that you could scrape carpet fluff from it and she lets rip with a string of expletives, so strong that they would even make the young Eddy Murphy blush, and then I know that now it's safe enough to suggest that maybe we could go out for something to eat, maybe try that Hawaiian place that has just opened up nearby. Hands on hips, Bonny laughs and says, okay as long as I change out of that dumb Speed Racer t-shirt that makes me look like a nerd. Anything you say, I reply and start to walk out of the room before stopping and saying that, shit, if the service in the restaurant is good today, I might even leave a tip.

Morning in the Park

by Sian Evans

The old man sits down on the park bench as the tour guide walks past with her group. "The park first opened in 1953," the woman begins, the man only half listening as through misted vision he watches a young couple kissing under the elm tree. "And was a favourite Saturday night spot for young lovers," he finishes on a whisper. His gaze soon returns to the sepia photograph that he holds between his gnarled fingers. "Sorry about the rain folks," she continues as the old man strokes his thumb over the face of a young woman smiling broadly as she leans against a tree trunk, "but we can't control nature now can we." A tear falls onto the photo; memories fading, dreams lost and years still left to live.

Silverio

by Diane Brady

He appears out of nowhere; turn around on any village road and watch him pass behind you, his steps too light to hear even though he walks with purpose. He's a magical little man with sad eyes, a Maya bush doctor -- healer of unknown talents -- often stooping to collect wild berries and seeds, roots and leaves along his path. In the forest a woman lies upon his altar of sticks, sweating with fever, moaning, the sores on her limbs so deep you can see through to her bones. He waves a handful of medicinal herbs grown along the mountain trail, eyes closed, swaying with the wind as he chants and sings, the birds silent, watching from the trees, even the insects respectful of his power. The ceremony continues after the skies darken and the moon rises; the woman's body, long passed to another world, cools and stiffens; tomorrow morning at dawn he will stand quietly beside her and swirl the brown elixir around and around in his mouth until it's bitterness overtakes him and he swallows. But tonight he is defeated, drunken with her memory – lost in the tradition and magic he hopes will save both of their souls.

Blue Smoke Pancakes

by Michael J. Killips

With all four burners on the stove pouring out the blue flame at full bore, the smell of breakfast and cigarettes is nearly as thick as the warm haze filling the simple, ample kitchen. Frantic activity is centered at the stove where Dot cooks the bacon crowded in the black, cast iron pan, sputtering and splattering grease in all directions. In a battered aluminum pot, the combination of hot water, a shovel full of white sugar and imitation maple flavor roll together to formulate what will soon pass for syrup. To keep the nearly tasteless pancakes from sticking to the hot griddle, Dot works up a dollop of sticky congealed bacon grease from a ceramic jar kept in the fridge. With a flick of the wrist, the grey goop drops off the serving spoon onto the cast iron griddle with a "pul-luck" and quickly transforms into a shiny liquid veneer and light blue smoke that rises to integrate with the kitchen's polluted atmosphere. Holding a cigarette in one hand and a spatula in the other Dot works the stove like a hardened assembly line worker, flipping, turning and stirring the raw ingredients into a meal that is consumed in a competitive, wordless flurry by her six hungry kids long before the pans cool.

A Wink and a Train Ride

by Lakin Khan

She could wink, I'll grant you that. Winked at the doorman, winked at the busboy, winked at the waiter, winked at the ticket clerk, winked at the conductor as he helped her up the three metal steps, winked at the dog curled up in the dirt on the shadow side of the depot. "Give a dog it's due," she said, winking at me from the rear platform of the Pullman, the fine red dust of the prairies staining her white sun hat, coating her toes and sandals. The train jerked, bells clanged, the conductor yelled "Alllllll aboooaarrd!" She leaned against the metal rail as the train pulled away; she opened her shoulder bag, a new one I suddenly realized, and flashed me the contents: bundles of bills, all the bills from the safe, I knew that instantly. No wonder she was winking.

Time Zones

by Tim Horvath

The clocks keep telling me what time it is all over the world— London , Tokyo , Brussels , Beruit, Sydney. But it's not the time I need; what I need is to know what I would be doing at this very moment in each of those places. But, you say, there is only one of you— well, that's easily circumvented. All I need to do is identify someone in each temporal sphere with a life similar enough to mine—wife with two sons, (elder one an undisputed success and younger one dangling between projects), steady position at a pharmaceutical firm, a full head of hair, tradeoff for nostril hair that grows in shanks, steady hand at darts, even liquor-addled, dark-haired chanteuse for a mistress (okay, I'm willing to be flexible on the hair color). This way, before proceeding, I could simply glance up at the wall and check out my counterpart in Brussels , my doppelganger in Berlin , my Viennese alter-ego, my long-lost twin in Bangalore , my shadow in Manila . How closely I'd scrutinize expressions and intonation, editing out the culturally specific and zooming in on the universal—the late-night phone manner, the surreptitious movements, the stashing of gifts, the blubbering of apologies, the way each version of me discretely switches one medication for another at that ungodly hour when all pills blur together, though elsewhere, needless to say, it is daytime.

The Dolls

by Alice J. Byrd

Since I was little, I've had a collection of porcelain dolls and they would stand on top of my bookshelves, peering at me through yellowing lace and from under gaudy plumed hats. I used to have nightmares about those dolls and their cold cheeks, their blank eyes framed by someone else's lashes, their perfect curls and full pouting lips. I would dream that I was trapped in porcelain, that I too was peering through glass eyeballs from the top of my bookcase. I couldn't move, or talk, or think – I could only exist, a fragile, hand-painted porcelain child frozen in perfection. When I woke up, I would cry with relief at the blood pounding in my temples, my trembling fingers, and my own eyelashes. Those nightmares have since given way to new ones, but I still have those dolls, and every time I see them I suppress a gasp and I wonder if there is someone in there, staring through glass pupils, voiceless.

Left Behind

by Melody Gray

I sat at the supper table listening to the basketball bouncing to the rhythm of my heartbeat as he came closer to my house. I was nine years old and he was the first boy to break my heart. He was not the most handsome boy in fifth grade with his beak-like nose and long lanky body, but he noticed me even when I was invisible to others. Then the new girl came to town and she was everything I wasn't; long blonde hair like wheat blowing in a field, funny, athletic, and most of all she could draw horses like an real artist. This new girl wanted to be my best friend, but I knew she could steal away what little I had in one breath. Silently I sat while my new friend fluttered her eyes and I watched my first crush slowly slip away from me, enthralled by this enchanted princess who swept him off his feet on her hand drawn horse leaving me behind.

Cleave

by Sarah Wallis

Our desires have an inner music – and that is all we have. The inner music of intuition, listening to who loves us, who loves us not? Who will advance and advise us- tell us when the student is ready the master will appear, skilled in the art of love. One who will recognize the swooning for what it is; the one pressed tight against the other. Cleaved together. Dancing their fingers and listening to the pattern of received blood, the surges of the heart thundering, and as much as their minds told them- this us is too fast, too strange...they could not stop themselves falling into each others arms, like something meant to be.

Rain Check

by Rod Drake

I noticed her on the other side of Market Street, that day in the downpour. She looked miserably wet and cold but flashed me a quick, fragile smile so beautiful that it momentarily lit up the otherwise dismal day. I wanted to cross over and meet her, but the steaming traffic prevented that. So instead I shadowed her down the block until she ducked into an eight-story apartment building. I stood aimlessly looking at the building, getting drenched, until I saw her body hit the pavement. She had apparently gone up to the roof and jumped; I wondered if her smile meant 'help me before it's too late' or simply 'see you later.'

Sanity First

by Mel George

I am a grown woman, yet today a hundred nannies have helpfully hemmed me in with advice. I have been cautioned that my hot drink may be hot; I have been taught how to sit on a chair; I have been warned of a potentially slippery floor; I have been told to take care on the escalators. Somebody thought fit to advise me not to shove my ankle down the small gap between the train and the platform. After work, I crossed the rail bridge to find that the yellow painted letters screaming DO NOT RUN on every step had been complemented by new signs next to the hand rail reading, 'Please use the hand rail'. Something like The Rage came over me and I leapt down those stairs two at a time, landed with a firm thud on both feet, and glared at the ticket man triumphantly. In that moment, my smugness evaporated into a kind of sad wonder – that it had become possible for me to actually feel like a devil-may-care rebel by proving to a stranger that I could use the stairs.

Minicab Driver

by Julian Baker

Yes, the money was good he thought. Living here as an economic refugee. But it was always raining, it was pouring down now. Waiting at the lights, with windows wound up. The car heater on full blast, drying the mud on the passenger's shoes, sitting beside him, a gift fruit basket wrapped in cellophane on her lap. He was momentarily happy; suddenly it smelt of home.

Funeral

by Patrick Salmon

The funeral guests hadn't worn enough black and wanted to leave too quickly. They shuffled about in intentionally uncomfortable shoes. Hoping to avoid any guilt when they didn't offer to help clean, they ignored the refreshments. Owen needed them to stay in his house longer. His sister, who had slept on the couch since his wife had died, was ready to go home tonight and leave him all alone. As he mingled with the crowd in his living room, he overheard as they practiced on each other excuses he knew they had in mind for him.

To My Local Newspaper

by David Holzel

For months now the majority of the letters you've published have been from readers announcing with much agitation that they are sick and tired and are cancelling their subscription. They all seem to have compelling reasons: either a story that appeared on the front page below the fold should have appeared above the fold or a story that appeared above the fold should not have appeared at all given that we are fighting two wars, a recession, Darfur and the resurgence of Britney Spears or because a story that deserved to be on the front page was buried deep inside the paper on that page that somehow doesn't get printed on or is smeared black with ink so there's nothing to read or that publishing photos of Barack Obama in swim trunks was inappropriate or that publishing photos of Barack Obama in swim trunks once again displays your pro-Obama bias and should have been accompanied by a photo of equal size of Sarah Palin in a bathing suit. I have read these letters and, because I disagreed with all of them – particularly the pedantic ones that try to emasculate you by pointing out that flaunt doesn't mean the same thing as flout – I have not cancelled my subscription. But recently I have noticed a disturbing trend: the percentage of letters announcing subscription cancellations is plummeting. You don't seem to get it – *readers want to read letters from readers who are canceling their subscriptions.* No wonder newspapers are dying; I am canceling my subscription.

I've Been Waiting for This Moment

by Alyssa Ning

It's been 7 months since I last walked through these doors. And even longer since I last saw you, 11 weeks longer to be exact; but who's counting? Well, me, I guess. I've also imagined what this reunion would be like, plotted it out in my head too many times, from the clever exchanges to my nonchalant body language. I might also be scared. Terrified.

The Storm Door

by Tara Lazar

"If he rings the bell, keep the storm door locked, tell him to take the letter in the mailbox and leave. Don't let him in, Kate, do you understand me?" Kate's mother returns to bed and the young girl sits on the stairs, elbows on knees, chin on fists, watching the door. The bell rings and Kate pleads with him. *Take the letter and leave, take the letter and go, you can't come in, she doesn't want you here, leave us alone, just go away.* When he punches through the screen, her mother appears at the top of the stairs, sobbing: "Let him in, Kate, for Christ's sake, let him in!"

Shelly and the Painted Desert

by Brian Steel

His boots scratched the gravel behind her and she heard the spit of his tobacco hit the hot, asphalt road with a dull splat; "How'd it get so many colors?" he asked in his usual, flattened tone. She turned slowly and saw him staring at the ground around his feet, then turned her head back to the tapestry of the landscape and replied with a sigh, "time, honey; time and weather and death; this whole place was once a giant forest with all kinds of animals and plants and birds, and they all died, like everything's got to, and then they got trapped in the soil, and time and the wind and the sun baked the whole dead forest into all these barren hills and made all these beautiful colors." She could feel him nodding silently behind her, mulling over her perfectly reasonable explanation, wondering whether to believe her or not; waiting, while she stared at the windswept bands of pink and blue, and orange and brown, that ran along the hills and valleys of the Painted Desert, like thousand-year-old ribbons melting into one another and fading to wasted pastels in the face of an unforgiving sun. "Kinda amazing isn't it?" she asked, "that so much dead stuff could create such a beautiful view on such a barren place," and she closed her eyes as a warm breeze swept up from the canyon below, gently licking strands of hair across her forehead. "Come on Shell, let's go," he said, "I'm hungry." She stared straight ahead at the painted rocks below, which seemed to glow in the distance of the afternoon, and moved her hands slowly over her flattened belly, whispering to herself, "So am I, dear, so am I."

A Little Too Soon

by Eric Kramer

Everything was going better than I could have hoped; the restaurant was exceptional, the movie pulled at your heartstrings, and the convenience store had a condom dispenser. A bottle of wine, two glasses, and a candle waited for us when we got back to my apartment. We sipped at the wine, laughing and talking into the early hours, and by the grace of God moved into the bedroom to consummate the evening. As matters began to grow more intense that uncomfortable sensation kicked in, going and coming as it always does as I silently attempted to control it, letting her think everything was moving along according to plan. I tried to fight as much as my will power would allow, reminding myself what the doctors told me would help and trying to think of anything less appealing, however all hope was lost with a gasp and a whimper. I tried subtly to distract her, however she had already reached for my boxers to see that, to my dismay, underneath my fruit of the looms rested the fruit of my loins.

Vanity

by Mindy Munro

I heard the word "cancer" for the first time in regard to my personal health exactly ten days before my thirty-eighth birthday. Two weeks later, a surgeon removed my thyroid gland and what he later told me was a cancerous mass; a one-and-a-half centimeter tumor filled with follicular carcinoma. When I returned home from the hospital I spent hours looking into the mirror, ashamed of my own vanity, less afraid of the diagnosis than what I saw staring back at me. A stiff row of stitches three inches long was sewn across the base of my throat, there were bruises on both of my arms, swollen veins on my hands, and sticky black lines where adhesive tape had held everything in place on the outside while I fell apart on the inside. I watched my reflection swallow. I was not yet brave enough to press my fingers to the place where the lump used to be.

Glass Wax

by Craig Daniels

Like guys do, he hoped he was mistaken, wishing he felt nothing at all. He walked faster to escape the feeling of being sorry for hurting her, sorry once again he didn't listen. On the park bench he sat to examine why the usual tricks of denial and stuffing those odd conglomerations deeper were not working. "What's going on," he plaintively asked, "why does she expect so much," he dribbled outlook but could not or would not answer his own question. Quietly the moment of introspection faded and he walked home. She kissed the glass in the window, placing a candle to light his way.

Voice

by Peter Holm-Jensen

It's your own, it's you and not you, babbling on day and night in a lunatic monologue. A man muttering in a room, a man and his skull, a man in his skull, a man carrying around his skull, babbling on. Repeat, cease, start, forget, remember, circle, abandon, stop, continue. Prodded into speech, prodded and prodder. Love it or hate it it's there either way. Sometimes it seems it could go on without you, a babble with a voice of its own, warring with its own words.

Chance

by austere seeker

She'd seen it coming for long now, just quicksilver images that she'd greedily snatch from the ether; rough footsteps thundering on the carved staircase, the woman fleeing in a chiffon saree embroidered with swarovski crystals, screams, shattering glass, rat-a-tat of gunfire, the chandelier in the Crystal Room swinging as a volley of bullets hit it. But there was no continuity, it didn't make sense, not really; so she snipped away and parceled bits and pieces in story after story that she wrote up and filed to the kind writing group across the seas, all apple pie and sunshine; here a nit, there a tweak, sentence construction, tense and verb, very nice, looks good, thank you. Week after week, word count to a four hundred. Until that shocking dawn when she stared at an angry sms bleary eyed, "What is happening to Bombay?" Over the next 60 hours she sat channel dazed, awash in a flood of twitter alerts, trying not to think of the carpeted wooden stairs, the way the light fell upon the sea and the rock solid Gateway; the glass-paneled ballroom that once played host to company princes, statesmen and royals, and the many who were surely trapped moth-like in that hellman's sights, like the lady in a purple crystal-embroidered saree. That was the last she'd write of danger, grenades explosions, acrid smoke and gunmen for a while, she promised herself, simpering starlets and financial scoundrels were a way better bet.

Winter Morning

by James Simpson

He could learn nothing from the expression on her face because he'd always had trouble reading faces other than happy or sad, and hers was an utter blank to him now. Maybe she was just in a very deep sleep. He signed; really, he knew. This was the day they'd talked about, usually after dinner so as not to spoil his appetite with worrying. He would miss her terribly, but he also knew he wouldn't cry. Her eyelids didn't even flutter when he pulled back the covers, so he reached out and laid his hand on her cheek which was as cold and firm as the ground outside.

Part 4

Uncle Sammy's Barber

by Pamila Payne

His hair was all wrong. It was stuck down flat on his head without a single rumple, and it didn't poof a bit. She shook her head sadly and tsk, tsked as she pulled her comb out of her purse and commenced to do him right. She knew just how to make him look real nice, 'cause she'd been his barber for, oh... a long, long time. Gramma's scream liked to scare the pants off of her and she dropped her comb in the casket when Grampa grabbed her, hauled her off the chair and carried her out of the funeral parlor. She regretted the spanking she knew was coming, but looking over her grampa's shoulder at Uncle Sammy lying in his casket, she was pleased to see his white, fluffy hair sticking up nice and high, just the way he'd always told her he liked it.

Fast Learner

by Libby Sumner

My back arched as the flogger landed on it once again and I let out a soft whimper as his fingers curled into my hair and I felt his lips brush my ear as he asked if I was going to be a good little slave tonight. I shivered and nodded as he let go of my hair and scratched down my back to where my cuffs were joined. I moaned and pressed back against him as he ground teasingly against me and patted my hands before pulling me into a standing position. He nipped at my neck and pushed me toward the stairs leading up to the bedroom and then safely guided me up them. He chained me to the foot of the bed and tucked me in tenderly before laying a soft kiss on my forehead. My lips curled into a smirk as a thought floated across my mind before I contentedly drifted off to sleep, '*Damn*, he really *is* kinkier than I thought.'

The Train

by Jeanette Cheezum

I sit here rocking back and forth. The gentle sway of the train soothes me somehow at the evenings end. My mother's words are ever present "Don't wear revealing clothes, you must keep your hair pulled back and never, never use vulgar language. Be shy around the men, they like to feel in control. You don't need to go to college; household duties will bring you knowledge." There's a desperate looking man ~ one more trick before we stop yields money in my hand.

Goodbyes

by Shelly Rae Rich

Putrid smells come from the refrigerator and I scour myself with Comet. We had puppies the last time the dog went in heat, but now I've hammered the swinging doors shut for good. There seem to be cries that turn into smirky giggles every time I look at that door, expecting. But need is only want. Wanton candles of lust burn through the night but I am too busy picking flowers from the carpet. They can't survive underfoot.

Bookends (I)

by Linda Simoni-Wastila

Do I love you enough? You, the aftereffect of endless appointments and near-daily blood sticks, the needles' cross-hatches marking me a junkie of sorts; the disappointment of every failed implant only fueled my appetite for the next humiliating procedure under the tented sheet, legs parted wider than the jaws of life. You, my quarter-million dollar princess; you, whom I desired more than my soul, my marriage; you, who for years existed but in fantasy: your warm baby-powder body snuggling against my breast, lazy afternoons playing peek-a-boo in Indian summer leaves, the scent of your milk-stained breath... Now, your red face agonizes confusion, wanting food, wanting sleep, wanting, always wanting, your selfish wail pervades, your needy blue eyes follow; I can't shower, can't piss without you clinging to me. You have transformed me into an aimless, sleepless wraith pacing the endless hall and all I want is to slam you against the wall or hand you to a stranger, perhaps the woman who gazed longingly at you in the park, but I keep pat-patting, trying to get you to burp into the disgusting white flannel draped over my shoulder, my snotty badge of motherhood. Isn't this proof enough of my love?

Bookends (II)

by Linda Simoni-Wastila

Only the steady thump-thump of the hissing machine, valves pressing and depressing against your will, remind me you are here. Like you, I dress in white; like you, many patients call me angel and I guess I am, administering to their wounds and sighs and bedpans and now, ministering to you, embellishing the chart with your vitals, watching you waste to a shrunken, wheezing vessel. The clacking ventilator reminds me of the ice cubes rattling in your highball the nights I nagged you to stop, your hands jittering between the glass and the cigarette, but your yellowed fingers stabbed and twisted the butt into ashes, proving you did not love me - enough. You moan and turn your withered face to the weak gasp of winter sun bullying its way through the window. It's only a matter of time, I rationalize, and fiddle with the tubing, adjusting the flow. The morphine races down to the catheter in your wrist and I wonder: Mama, did I love you enough?

Somewhere in Alabama, Circa 2055

by Steven Kunert

The insects, new ones I ain't seen before, they're everywhere, and they killed one of the piglets, for food, I guess. The plastic wrap and foil stuffed around the doors and windows keep them out, mostly, but the cockroaches swarm up from under the floor. The cat had enough, I reckon, why I ain't seen him in over a month. Been at least two years since it rained more than I sweat, and the news people say the South lost near half its population, going here, going there, still blaming global warming, the dopes. My folks wouldn't believe these bugs—good thing they're dead. They always hated roaches the most.

RSVP

by Lauren Becker

Yes, I will come to your party. I will bring a bottle but will drink your cheap, watery margaritas. I will add extra tequila. I will talk to your brother. I will leave with your brother. Thanks so much for the invitation.

Sexy Sadie Saves Someone

by Daniel Stine

Sexy Sadie is speeding along highway 101 between San Francisco and San Jose, she's doing her nails and steering with her knee when a maniac in a Mazda mashes into a Montero, causing a pile up that pulls poor Sadie in and before she knows it she is upside down and spinning round and round and when she stops spinning she's facing almost directly into the windshield of the toppled Montero where a man lies unconscious. Cursing her newly painted, now broken fingernails she wrestles off the seat belt and drops to the top of her crashed up car and crawls out through the shattered glass, sliding up to the side and looking around for some sort of assistance when the Montero man starts screaming bloody hell, and bloody it was and Sadie hates the sight of blood but nobody was coming so Sadie had to act, she called 911 and got a hunk. Deep soothing-voiced hunk on the horn tells Sadie to describe what she sees and she does so drawing strength from his calmness and when the hunk tells her to go to the injured man in the Montero Sadie balks saying there is blood everywhere and it's making her sick but the honey-sounding hunk comforts her and tells her she has the right stuff and he tells her to go to the Montero man and stop the bleeding by any means, which she does by tearing off a piece of her slinky silk skirt and with the help of her hunky helper ties Montero Mans leg off with a tourniquet. With her new phone buddy purring sweet somethings in her ear Sadie is startled when the Montero man begins convulsing in canvas belts and his eyes are bulging and Sadie is terrified and she screams into the cell and like cool rain after a hot day the voice peacefully instructs the struggling Sadie to release the Montero man from his bondage and prepare for further instructions, which Sadie does after steeling her nerves with a dose of the hunk humming a relaxing tune and as Sadie pushes herself away from the man she is horrified to find blood on her hands and it's not his, it's hers and whoa, what's this, and out she goes. Lights on and Sadie's home, she awakens in a hospital bed surrounded by three, count them, three men and man number one is in bandages and even still he's pretty hot and man number two is wearing a white coat and man he's hot too and probably rich to boot and the third man is not so hot and maybe a little fat and all three men are smiling at sweet sexy Sadie as she tries to sit up and take stock of this interesting situation, but the stress is too much and out she goes, Sadie slips silently into deep sleep. Sadie doesn't know it but she seriously suffered in the accident and time is on leave as she stabilizes and when she's able to sit with out swooning she again holds court with the three hot men, well, two hot men and one not so hot, anyway Sadie smiles and the three men smile and eyes are bright and its clear a choice must be made and Sadie asks the men for their names, which they reply with hopes and dreams and Sadie is surprised to hear honey pour from man number three and suddenly its clear that the hotties can't hold a candle to her honey, not so hunky, helper for who else could make Sadie so strong?

Blameless

by James Simpson

I marvel at how different, in the simplest way, my daughter's childhood is than mine: in Florida I dreamed of northern snow, while here in New York she dreams of Florida and the beach. Of course, her image of Florida is an innocent one of sand and sun, for her life so far has been safe and comfortable, steady and uneventful. My Florida images often include days spent outdoors roaming the neighborhood beneath a relentless and white-hot sun, my mother returning home from work tired and sad. After my father left us, I tiptoed around my mother, wanting only to comfort her while keeping my distance. I explained to my friends in Miss Branch's 3rd grade that my mother and father no longer enjoyed the same things. Each day I told myself it was not because of me.

Winter

by Nicole Taylor

I am struck by the gentleness with which his calloused hand lingers upon my skin. Before he came here, to me, he worked eleven hour days on sun-battered Iranian farms. Lying beside him, the two of us illuminated by the weak winter light seeping through the window, I tutor him in English turns of phrase. I tell him, "The course of true love never runs smooth", a reference to his struggle to come to me here in New York, and he repeats my words in a steady and eager voice. He calls me his azizam, his sweetheart. This man has become a habit of mine.

Childless

by Zeptimius Hedrapor

The black-haired twin girls with bright blue eyes faced him as he sat down in the bus. They were in their early teens, and they were beautiful. Staring at them intently, he imagined them as his own, raising them, fussing over them, making them pancakes for Sunday breakfast. The girls, who looked as if he'd known them all his life, were talking to each other and didn't notice him. When he acknowledged to himself that he would die childless and would leave no progeny behind, his chest ached. As the twins reached their stop and got off, he reached the diagnosis that the pain must be caused by an excess of unused love, trapped inside him.

Pieces of You

by Mercedes M. Yardley

Every time that something dies, like grace or love or souls, they fall to the ground like stars. It's been happening more and more lately, and we run around covering our heads and screaming as the constellations crash around us. Here's something you need to know, though. I am not afraid. I picked up a small star years ago, and I'm holding it behind my back for that moment when the sky goes black and you're looking for something bright to hope for. I'll open my hands and show you that I have it, this last piece of you.

Vicarious

by Stephen J. Davis

I could hardly believe the permission my wife was granting me, "You know, if you want, you can have an affair." I was certainly tempted because ever since her accident Deadra's been suffering from complete paralysis. "Well," I say, "if it wouldn't bother you." And she confirmed that it wouldn't. So what I did was have molds made from all of Deadra's body parts, then with photographic aid, had them transformed into an anatomically correct doll. Soon enough I was making passionate love to my mistress while Deadra looked on, and I could tell, indeed, that my wife was aroused.

3117 7th Street North

by Lisa Miller

I was born and raised in the 1970's in Fargo. Yeah, like the movie, only less of the corny accent (and no wood chippers in the back yard), but complete with Germans, Scandinavian, and Irish who mixed and matched through marriages and business partnerships and farms bought and sold from one shrinking generation to the next because people stopped having 10 or 15 children – just in case – cutting back to 2 or 3 as they moved into the city for jobs. And you betcha we had green and rust colored shag carpet in the house, fondue parties, lefsa rolled up around butter and brown sugar for snacks, snow boots for every occasion, and enough of that Lutheran reserve to make us excellent neighbors who delivered casseroles to sick friends, and cookies to everyone at Christmas, but otherwise waited for an invitation to visit. I remember the smell of sugar beets being processed at the sugar beet plant on the edge of town, and dead fish shy and bloated on the golf course after the Red River flooded one summer, along with walking a few blocks to and from kindergarten and riding bikes with my sister to Harry Holland swimming pool on hot summer days. And when the couple two houses down divorced and moved away, it was a scandal discussed in low voices over backyard fences as the women of the neighborhood reaffirmed their belief that (somehow) Carol had betrayed them by signing those papers, packing up the kids and leaving, while the men left behind joked about Jerry's new bachelor pad and eyed their wives and kids as they weighed lives lived thus far. We lived in square houses surrounded by green squares of lawn with appropriate decorations for each holiday, we lived with fathers who worked 9 to 5 and mothers who drove American made cars, we lived with secrets we overheard from our beds at night as our parents watched Johnny Carson and talked, and we lived with parents who always maintained the façade that everything was all right.

Dream of Waking

by Kathryn Burkett

You can't wake up. You're beating behind your eyelids, trying to pry them open, thrashing wildly in your brain, but you can't wake up. What kind of dreaming is this? All you wanted was sleep, sleep, and now you have it. You're sleeping, just like you wanted, existing in blackness, and now you're terrified that you'll never be able to wake up. There is still light, if you can only open your eyes.

Just a Job

by Doug McIntire

The summer after college, I worked as a clerk in a liquor store on the outskirts of town. One morning I arrived to find a homeless man, dirty and disheveled, waiting patiently for the store to open. I remember thinking that he might be there to rob us, but when I opened the door at nine o'clock sharp, he just came in and asked for the cheapest pint of vodka we carried. His hands shook as he paid with loose pocket change and then picked up the small brown paper bag from the counter. Once outside, I watched as he opened the bottle, tipped it up and chugged it down, draining it in one long draw. That was the precise moment when I knew it was time for me to seek employment elsewhere.

315 is Stealing Cheese Again

by Linda Courtland

She spied the packets of cheese at the end of the buffet line, nestled between the yogurt tubs and hardboiled eggs. Standing with the hotel's other guests, who'd all been reduced to room numbers, 315 read the sign forbidding the removal of food from the dining area. She slid two orange squares into her purse anyway, embarking on a life of crime that could very well threaten her professional future. Hotel chains talk, of course, dishing about outrageous antics and exchanging surveillance footage of amateur cheddar thieves. 315 knew that bad things could happen in this city; she had grown up here. And between business meetings, she listened to her stomach growl and struggled to outrun the hungry echoes of her youth – an ultra-competent career woman trembling behind a massive desk and measuring her progress in pilfered packets of processed cheese.

Some Kind of Heaven

by Oceana Setaysha

On the eve of the Balinese New Year, before the silence of Nyepi wraps us up in nothingness to repair the imbalances of the world, we exorcise demons. In a frenzy of good intentions we all take to the dimly lit streets and sweat as one body while watching the parade of a thousand hand-made monsters. They loom above us, scraping the sky, and dance menacingly to the echoing sound of the gamelan over swaying palms. When they stop we swell and break ranks, an immovable wall of people, dancing, yelling and singing like tomorrow's never coming, and today is all we've got. Then, when the New Year dawns with an eerie silent shadow coating the tropical paradise, it is not the vast emptiness that makes us marvel. It is the feeling of sitting in the ringing quiet, full of awe, wondering if heaven is anything like this.

Alabama / The Other Side

by Christen Buckler

Because I am twenty-two and because I've never been anywhere besides where I always am, I decided to drive from Florida to Alabama. Sleep in a motel, maybe, or buy some souvenirs with a different state's name on it. So I load up my duct-taped car and head for the state line. I run out of gas in Dothan and fill up at a Wal-Mart. And I stand in the parking lot and stare at the sky and think about how much Alabama looks like Florida, with a couple of different license plates. And the grass is brown now, but I bet in the spring it'll be green again.

Lava Woman

by Belinda Subraman

She wanted to climb the volcano. She wanted to look down into the cone and see molten red bubbling beneath the surface. It was not enough to be in a tropical paradise, she had to live dangerously. She had to be where trees are like match sticks. She knew if she was close enough to see the lava and it toppled over the cone there was no way she would outrun the flow. She chanced another way of being in nature, of being a component in lava rock, or if there was no overflow that day she would live to climb other hot mountains.

There Must Be Something to Say, Eh?

by Allan Revich

The other day this guy I know was talking to me. He was rambling on and on about something or another. His drivel was driving me mad. I started to daydream while he was yammering away. When he asked me what I thought, I just answered, "I dunno, what do you think?" That seemed to be enough for him.

My Brother was Music

by Christopher Cocca

In the quiet between highway ribs we were made as brothers; between home and home again the quiet made us. There is no one, now, who knows what I can say to fear, fears of calm and quiet that make boys men and fathers. On public radio from private city schools they are talking about art and peace and craft with righteous elocution. But you spoke like songs and sung like land. Here, you kept me honest-brother, you were music. I wonder if you'd hate this.

Snacks

by Christine Hamm

Please don't cannibalize each other, Sally writes, *if your car gets stuck in snow on the way to Connecticut.* I think about the Saturn, how some of the doors won't open since the accident last Fall. There was another woman in his car then, one who spoke his version of Chinese, one who liked to take pictures of herself in a darling Santa's cap next to national monuments. She was ten years younger than me, *a friend*. My stomach still shrinks to a fist when I find him on the phone, apologizing again for *swerving to the left*, though she only cut her elbow, a minor scratch. I write Sally back, promising to stock canned tomatoes and pears in the back seat, just in case.

Fetish

by Sherrie Pilkington

It was that glorious time of year with warm breezes and warmer temperatures; the resurrection of new life and the perfect time to give in to her annual craving. She grabbed him securely with both hands; his blank stare was the invitation she needed to remain detached from such an adorable face. Without hesitation she bit down into his ear letting the smooth sweetness spread across her tongue. Next she gnashed her teeth against his eyes raking them from their perch. Unabashedly she removed his nose and savored the delectable moment as its flavor exploded in her mouth. Self gratification never felt so good as she secretly gave thanks for chocolate Easter bunnies.

This Time, I Won

by Caren Coté

The little girl, she couldn't be more than two, toddles along the grass near the top of the hill, uneven footing or her beginner status sending her to the ground on her well-padded bottom every few steps. Her mother retrieves her before she wanders far but the little girl in the pink dress and matching hat sets out again, single-minded as only toddlers can be, toward the ducks eating from a pile of dog food nearby. She doesn't cry when instead of regaining her feet she manages to start herself rolling down the hill. Despite the gentle slope she picks up speed at an alarming rate. Before I can move or her mother notice what's happening she's plunked into the duck pond as smoothly as a piece of firewood. She coughs once and then smiles after I fish her out; her mother glares at me for paying more attention to her daughter than she had, but I don't mind.

Skinny Jeans

by Nicole Roura

And no, I'm not talking about the unisex trend that we have resurrected. I'm talking about those golden age pair of jeans that sit in your drawer, tormenting you with reminders of your tiny twenties. The pair that accented all the right curves in all the right places. The pair that you somehow put on a little too much weight to squeeze into, turning , suddenly, from your "golden" jeans to your "goal" jeans (as soon as you shed those few pounds). And now, after quite some time, quite regrettably, and absolutely broken-heartedly, the pair that you must pass on to someone else as the "go-ahead-and-take-away-my-youth" jeans. Yep, *those* skinny jeans - you know you own a pair of those.

Punishment for What?

by Sian Evans

There is a hard seat beneath me and the crisp packet at my feet catches the rain, but these irritants today are of little consequence as I came here to be alone with my thoughts. I'm a good person and I'm ill, the tests results are not back yet so I don't know if I'm dying. People die everyday; men, children, women, children, even dogs and I never think about them, it shames me to know that. I'm a good person, so what happens if I don't like the people in Heaven? Dostoevsky says that Heaven might be *a small room – a bathroom, if you will – blackened by smoke, with spiders in every corner, supposing that to be eternity.* There is a hard seat beneath me and I am alone with my thoughts; for now that is my eternity.

Winter Storms

by Juliana Perry

This year the pipes froze while the creditors called day by day, a plumber came in the night and left without charging, and the old man shipped gifts to the children. As the time flies by our un-expecting minds, how will we carry on and leave behind moments and memories that hurt us? Would it be as simple as writing about that pain and letting go? Playing house while maintaining family, work and friends has become an odd challenge, still trying to let go and release the vice on my chest in order to accept the box from out of town, wrapped with duct tape and filled with three unwrapped stuffed animals. Knowing that the heart from whence they came is shriveled and hard, this is a huge offering, the first in four years, I will set aside that knowledge with the collector's bills, the plumbing and indecision on my part. As striving for family can be joyful it also causes pain; the truth here is the striving to accept has not stopped yet.

Born Under a Bad Moon

by Heather Leet

My grandmother always said I was born under a bad moon. Every time she visited me she would give me some sort of trinket to ward off the evil she said surrounded me. I did not have the strength to tell her I liked the evil. I liked the feel of it as it wrapped itself around me and made my heart pound with desire for all the things I knew were bad. The night she died I felt it in my bones as slowly the evil swirled away and my heart felt light for the first time. Grandmother had been wrong, I was not born under a bad moon; she was.

At His House

by Timothy Gager

Their lovemaking was savage. It was the way a knife slices through a red bell pepper. They fucked while the onions caramelized, then became burnt. The road back to work had started to ice; one false slip from the tire's firm edge to the bald middle tread would send them through a guardrail. We can't do this anymore, she said. He noticed tears never freeze.

Back to Earth

by Ian Rochford

Stanley had always thought it preposterous that technologically advanced aliens would cross galaxies just to probe the anal canals of human beings. Until it happened to him. The alien held a black, glassy pea between his fingers. "You should be grateful - we have a need for this, the rarest and most valuable substance in the universe, and now your prostate works properly." "You should pay me for that, I've been violated and plundered, and... and... *I could sue you!*" complained Stanley. "Be thankful we're repatriating you, instead of just ejecting you, Monkey-Man," the Alien growled, shoving his silvery face into Stanley's and baring formidable teeth, "and that I personally consider you inedible... and unattractive."

Jaded

by Jasmin Guleria

She woke up the next morning in the best type of pain. Her lips were raw from kissing, and her cheeks were flushed a deep pink. Her chin and nose were scratched from his scruffy prickly beard, that rubbed over her face as he reached for her mouth. Her stomach had scratches from where his hands had reached and pulled at her clothing until all that was left to pull was skin, her hair was a tangled flash of crazy and her eyes sparkled with morning after delight. Her years with men in this city had made her accustomed to one-night wonders thus making her void of expectations; when he called the next day she was too shocked to answer the phone and his sweet message asking her to lunch was met with an opened mouthed gape of disbelief. She deleted his number from her phone, and avoided places she knew he would be; too jaded by the city's trash to believe it could contain any sort of treasure.

A Note to Me

by Donna Martines

If I could do this all over again, I'd sit myself down at sixteen and tell me that it gets worse before it gets better unfortunately. You will spend a lot of time being lazy, then you will be very ambitious... you'll be really ignorant for awhile too, however don't worry... you'll finish off smarter than most everyone. Don't get upset when you do poorly on your first Art History exam, look too fat in those jeans, the doctor finds a lump in your breast or when that Italian jerk doesn't call... and never let her make you feel any less than you are... because you are more valued than most. Myself, you just have to believe me. You'll get to a day when you're the best at what you do, price tags won't matter, you'll have too many best friends and meeting your hero will come as no surprise. And myself, never forget that fulfillment in your life comes from what is important to you and not to someone else... if there is anything I could teach me, it's this.

My Jacket

by Prachi Jain

I was reading a book in the library with my back to the wall. "Excuse me," he asked, "how much does that jacket cost?" I made a dour face when I took off my jacket and saw that it was smeared with fresh white paint off the wall. "I will pay for the jacket or at the very least reimburse you for the dry-cleaning." Writing his address on a piece of paper he continued, "that is my punishment for not putting up a 'wet paint' sign here." Most of the paint came off in the wash but two days later I met his unrecognizing gaze in a fancy downtown café, I realized I should have hit him with my jacket's dry cleaning bill.

Blackberry

by Tess Dickenson

The rich indigo juice staining her fingers brought decades-old memories of the laughter they shared as they climbed the hill, hand in hand, seeking the fullest, most promising bramble with its treasure trove of plump berries, guarded by a militia of well-honed thorns. The race to fill baskets to the brim, the need to be the champion of the berry-pickers, the smell of the baking bread made from their harvest...these things all raced through her mind in a panorama of color, sound and feeling. The thoughts of him...her brother...came so clear and so strong, carried on the scent of the berry. The moments shared that in another time joined souls now caused a break so clear that its edges sliced the heart. The picture in her mind shifted to fill with the memory of his back as he walked away. All this joy, all this pain, carried innocently in the decadent taste of blackberry...the taste of what might have been.

Part 5

The New Engagement Ring

by Ryan Ridge

He decided to propose during intercourse. Here's what he proposed: "How about I take this thing off, baby?" She slid him out, "If by 'take that thing off' you mean 'marry me', then yes, proceed." He thought about it. He supposed condomless sex was the new engagement ring, or maybe he'd heard that on the radio or read it on the Internet. He couldn't remember, but he proceeded anyway—all the way to the altar.

Truth Hurts

by Quin Browne

Without the formality of the salute, they moved into place, fencers in their final match, squaring off when he came to get his things--his portion of their life together. Engaging in conversation, words their rapiers, parrying... advance... retreat; her pain at being found wanting like a stone bruise; invisible, yet, far too tender to the touch. She feinted, saying in a low voice how confident he'd become since he'd met his lover. Flustered, flattered, preening... his defense dropped, asking why did she think so. Executing a fast riposte, serene smile in place, she struck the winning touch, "Because every time you fuck her, you boldly go where so many have gone before." He gazed dully at the closed door, his hand reaching up to stroke his face, seeking traces of blood from where his ego had been nicked.

Food Fallout

by Jessica Patient

The medias 'obesity time bomb' never ignited and exploded. It became a redundant bomb just like the World War II bombs that need deactivating when a retired gentleman has been over zealous with digging in the garden and the army has to come trampling through the living room with their muddy boots to deactivate, take away and dispose of the relic. Food just stopped arriving on the supermarket shelves, making till-girls unnecessary and trolleys were abandoned in empty, derelict car parks. Helpless scientists sat on the sidelines: shrivelled seeds, cracked earth, blazing summers, monsoon winters. The population withered like failing crops – drooping but trying to sustain on rain, soil and rodents but slowly the animals vanished. Vegetation didn't flourish or grow back. And that was when the bodies started pilling up.

Separation

by Jeanette Cheezum

I have to admit it amazes me how much time and money she can spend on frivolous things. Of course she loves a good party and to put on airs, it's all for show and the country club set. If they only knew how neurotic she is and how poorly... we really get along. I have to keep her on a short leash — if there are any attractive women in the room and they're near me — she becomes insanely jealous. I don't feel guilty anymore; I've done nothing wrong. It's going to be difficult for her when the moving truck arrives and only my things are loaded.

Biopsy

by Tovli Simiryan

I often hear a voice moving like a whisper down a corridor decorated with dark red bricks where kittens chase our shoelaces, then scamper into the sun. Letter by letter it calls for the air to make ripples, a soothing correction of imbalance and devotion that carves a path for dreams that taste of memory, yet ascend along a dark horizon turning stories into daylight. In our time they often speak of needles puncturing disease, hoisting evil from a vein without leaving marks or permanency of any sort. Occasionally, malevolent and grainy tissue is mistaken as shadow and their roots are left behind to fester, causing the sky to fold like a dead rose unable to re-seed, or attach itself to the next day. When this happens, delightful prayer, words and little pieces one dislodges from the depths of a pocket will not help, or predict the ounce of survival that smoothes wrinkles from the soul. It's then kittens jumping into setting stars create a worthy seam, whispers matter and the path begins as darkness, just below an odd, but lasting sigh.

The Story Teller

by Kevin Michaels

I would read her stories on quiet summer days as we sat along the river, just the two of us stretched out in the tall grass, hidden in the shade of the pine trees lining the banks of the Mullica while a gentle breeze cooled our skin. She liked the way I read to her and said it wasn't just the stories but the sound of my voice – how I would give some words little twists of emotion, along with the emphasis I put on certain sentences to make them stand out, and I loved the way Katie would giggle when I mispronounced the vocabulary words we had learned in Miss Rittenberg's English class only weeks earlier. Her body would sway slowly from side to side before she dropped her head in my lap, closing her eyes to listen as I read; the hours and days that passed never mattered back then, neither one of us ever imagining we could run out of time or that it would pass so quickly. Some days we dreamed about a world beyond the Mullica and our little New Jersey town - as the years went by we talked about a life together and a world waiting to be explored; Katie would take my hand in hers as I told another story about the places we could go and smile at the depth of my ambition and the strength of our growing love. Now, I am left to fill our days with stories about the places we have visited while wishing that for a little while we can return, if only in our dreams - some times for just a few moments my words unlock a memory long since buried and her eyes light up with a recognition that is both rare and fleeting. All I can do is hope that the next time I read to her I will again see that glow in her eyes and the spark that lights up her expression when she briefly remembers the life and the love we have shared.

Bird Man

by Belinda Subraman

He was at the top of the Eiffel Tower, far above the elevator shaft, nearing the utmost point. He dreamed of wings as his arms took flight. He caught himself like a bird of prey feeding on steel. His feet never left their perch but swiveled with the fall. Just before his head would have smashed into the girders his backpack filled with blankets and pillows cushioned the blow. Photographers plastered his face all over the journals, calling him "Bird Man of Eiffel," saying he had lived to crow about his ascent.

Clemency

by Sarah Wallis

I saw the gold band after my heart had planned you, my thoughts seduced you. It was no trick, there was a connection, present in the play of delighted eyes under candlelight, and the draw of a magnet pulling us together. We made subtle smiles, drifting closer as two boats bobbing the tide. We were almost innocent over drinks, a brush of colliding fingertips as we talked with our hands, demonstrating emphasis to the air. When the end of the evening could no longer be prolonged in the bar, we finally fell into silent gazes and threaded our violent hopes together. At this point, it should have been sooner but your eyes were irresistible, I realised the meaning built into a twist of gold and begged forgiveness for the empty castles I had almost built there.

Slightly Speckled

by Emily Anne Epstein

I was wearing shoes from the fifties and sweating down the streets of Buenos Aires when I didn't get her email. I had the ticket in my hand and I was on my way to Spanish class and then the Craigslist Thanksgiving. It wasn't going to be pretty. The redhead said it would be all right. She came in yellow sunglasses, a red purse and a blue necklace; that black dress, high waist. Was it those freckles or faint blue eyes?

Directions to My House

by David Gianatasio

Turn left at the intersection where the 2nd set of lights used to be, at the entrance to the rendering plant, before they tore it down and made the whole strip a "Green District" and built all those malls. There's a rotary, I think, but I've never understood how those work, and the one I'm thinking of might only exist in my mind, so it's probably best to avoid the rotary altogether -- or else bear right. If you get lost, do NOT stop and ask for directions; the people around here will just roll their eyes, clench their fists and mutter in a language only they can understand. If things begin to look reassuringly familiar, you're gone too far. These aren't very good directions. But that's OK: my house isn't here anymore.

No Entry / No Exit

by Caroline Wells

I hear the front door open; the alarm sounds momentarily then quickly stops, alerting me she is home. My queasiness begins as I listen to her climb the stairs and quietly close her door. After several minutes, the urge overtakes me, and I walk to her room; four light taps tell her it's me. "What?" is the cue that allows me to open her door, but the low, flat tone of her voice answers all I need to know. Her beauty sometimes startles me, and I watch as she assesses herself in the mirror, her revulsion blinding me like a halogenic glow. "I just wanted to make sure you were home," I lie, as I slowly step out, knowing her self-loathing needs a privacy I could never penetrate.

Wild Dinosaurs in the Backyard

by Adam J. Whitlatch

I can hardly remember a time when I could leave the house without checking the windows first, carefully examining the trees for the slightest rustle of leaves or even the smallest flock of startled sparrows, not to mention I always feel silly creeping across the lawn with that damned .22 rifle clutched in my hands - it might as well be my son's Daisy air rifle for all the good it would do me; what I wouldn't give for a nice, heavy elephant gun. . . or a bazooka. It's all *NuGen Concepts*' fault - the bastards - their scientists discover a foolproof method of recovering prehistoric DNA from the fossilized remains of extinct animals and what do they do? They patented the DNA and made household pets out of the goddamned things - *that's* what they did! Oh, it was cute at first, all rainbows and sunshine - the newest holiday sensation: "Real Live Dinosaurs. . . a Triceratops for little Bobby and a cuddly Parasaurolophus for Suzie," but then like pet alligators being flushed down the toilet when the little darlings got too big for the garage or started eating the family dog they had to go. . . thousands of these genetically engineered dinosaurs being dumped into the wilds of America - including my back yard! So now here I am, tiptoeing across the road toward the mailbox with this pathetic little pea shooter clutched in my sweaty palms, looking over my shoulder at the tree line when suddenly a passing big rig blows its air horn at me - pulling me out of my bout of paranoia and leaving me clutching my heart, breathing heavily and trying to force the pounding organ back into my chest where it belongs. Then I hear it. . . at first I think it's another big rig until I recognize it for what it is: the trumpeting roar of an adult Tyrannosaurus Rex.

Marriage

by Julian Baker

Her father died when she got married. Literally, he expired between the altar and the door. People still occasionally asked her if perhaps halting the ceremony could have saved him. And she recounts that when she rushed to his side as the heart-attack struck, standing there waiting to give her away, he had wanted the wedding to go on. Between gasps he spoke quietly of rather dying happy now, seeing her marry, than risk his last few minutes and "miss his dream for his little girl". As he looked up his ashen face told of his certainty in the latter coming true, given the time the ambulance would take compared with finishing the service, so she said the only words she could. "I will... I do..."

Finally Free

by Lisa Reynolds

She sat at the table, her eyes puffy and red from the thousands of tears she cried over the man who didn't deserve them. Years of abuse beating down on the very core of her soul, finally coming to an end as she held the finalized divorce decree. She had a rush of emotions coursing through her with such speed and force that she felt momentarily disoriented. What to do now, she thought to herself. The possibilities were limitless as she started her list; take a cruise, go camping, take an art class, visit Disneyland, go to the beach, go dancing or just visit friends. "It doesn't matter what I do", she thought as she smiled, "for now I am finally free".

Tangled

by Jodi MacArthur

Everything is a tangled mess, the gold chain, knotted, on the table, my hair, unkempt, around my face, my heart, bleeding with the truth, the second I touched my true love's gift. Was it just yesterday that I beheld the magnificent creature in the wooded clearing? Its soft nostrils, breathing, breath into my hair, its fur coat, warm snow, between my fingertips, its golden horn, innocent and pure, glistening as the sun. I know now whose footsteps I heard, ran from, not wanting to bring harm to the coveted creature. "A golden chain for my true love's throat," he had said, bowing and presenting me with a dainty satin purse. Can I accept the chain and marry, knowing from what it is cast, or can I decline the blood offering, and lose my true love – I am a maiden no more.

Crushed

by Ryan W. Bradley

I was an ugly boy, and you were so incredibly perfect. The most beautiful girl an eleven-year-old boy could imagine. Against all odds you walked with me on the field trip, even held my hand, sweaty and shaking. I slipped my hand away a few times to wipe it on my jeans, but you didn't take notice, only kept your hand in the air between us, waiting for mine to return. And your laugh, the way your neck stretched elegantly, and your ponytail flittered buoyantly at the back of your head. Well, it was all of these things that crushed me.

My First Love

by Jillian Parker

Here is a confession: once, I had an illicit love affair, with a city of shadows. There was a time, when wisps of my soul shot up the Ostankino Tower, bounced off the nearest sputnik, and landed anywhere, everywhere, in all wheres that were Moskva; and the city, when I knew her, was drab and dull, in the only shades that Communism allowed. She was dingy and dusty, rickety and rusty, but oh, how I loved her, she-- she was my drug, my obsession; I memorized the names of her streets, and inscribed her metro map like hieroglyphics into the pan of my brain. Every underground station, from Kuzmin'ki, to Rechnoi Vokzal, hummed with the elixir of our crushing embrace. Now she is changed; the streets have been re-named, the facades restored, rings of highways now encircle her, countless rubles have been poured into her to soothe her roughness, to soften the edges, making her more pleasing to the taste of the *nouveau riche*. But until some rogue earthquake tumbles all of her towers towards her countless catacombs, a part of my heart will always be there, beating just beneath the crumbling tiles of a Khruschevka; I will weep when she weeps, I will dance when she dances, and if an iron fist tightens around her, I will ache with her in her anguish... moya Moskva.

Imagination

by Peter Holm-Jensen

She woke up, started drinking and sometime later went to bed having done something embarrassing. That was her life. They said she was spiritually broke, they told her to experiment with optimism. Was that some kind of joke? She replaced them with figures from her imagination and gave them all different names. Then she realized she could do the same with herself: she could recreate herself, change herself for the better.

Details

by Bruce Weber

looked for god in the details today. after attending emerson lecture at the university. seems like ralph was a pretty good guy. not as poetic as his protégé thoreau though. fell asleep a couple of times. woke up and pulled out my magnifying glass and started inspecting things "up close."

Games

by Ravi Mangla

She needs to know that passing Go doesn't constitute a new beginning. It's the same story each time around, the same avenues and stations. She thinks that just because we found the candlestick in the billiard room the mystery is solved. There's still the matter of who to blame. For every ladder up, there are two slick reptilian backs waiting on one errant step. Our battleship sunk a long time ago, and sorry won't change a thing.

The Conservationist

by Kim Tairi

Using the edge of the surgical blade with precision, Eva removed a flake of corrosive copper sulphate that was eating away at his sleek torso and after six torturous months removing layers of copper and zinc from his face she was excited about working on the rest of his body. Smiling to herself she noted how his fine Hellenistic features were much clearer now, you could even see his philtrum, suddenly she was overwhelmed by a desire to kiss him lightly on the mouth, to taste his sharp metallic lips. It was ridiculous but she suspected that she was in love with the statue and as the only metals conservationist in the museum, nearly every waking hour was spent in returning the bronze of the young, athletic Greek god to its former glory and her obsession was growing. Several hours of meticulous and painstakingly slow work with the microscope and the scalpel made her muscles ache, arching back to stretch she lightly rested her hand on his bicep... my god is that a pulse? Anxious, she turned to look at his face for reassurance, bright green eyes stared up at her, miraculously, he was coming to life and Eva was paralysed with fear, what the hell 's going on? Then he smiled up at her, she relaxed slightly, but as his lips drew further back revealing his teeth, each one filed to a point, Eva realised he wasn't a god - he was a demon.

Mother Tongue

by Benjamin Robinson

The extent of her appetite for possession was revealed in the marmalade debacle. One New Year's Eve she broke into the larder and ate his entire supply for the coming year. Three hundred and sixty five servings in a single sitting. She left no sign of crumbs. No interlocutor between desire and fruition, no intermediary for her stolen communion. He returned to find her face and neck glazed with the remnants, muttering indecipherable victories in a daze of stolen mornings.

The Six

by Rebecca Jane

The six members of the Pan family lived in a 1920s craftsman-style home that overlooked Sunset Cliffs. Each member lived a double life. Gramps survived Red Guard persecution, pledged loyalty to Communists, and later regulated nuclear plants for the unsuspecting Feds; Granny knitted imitations in a secret naughty nighty factory and ran a booming takeout chain on the side; Papa collected blood money from a banned-books smuggler, which supplemented his income as C.O.O of El Dorado Contracting Co. but then he was also slapped with his mistress's credit card debt; Mama disguised her voice for a 1-800 hotline six days a week and directed a church choir on Sundays; Sassy Pan hid in the nodding needlegrass to masturbate but donned an orange vest when on duty as School Crossing Guard; finally, Baby Pan woke and slept, woke and slept, woke and slept. The day after the vote on Proposition 5, a suit-and-tie Buildings Department man knocked on their front door and waved a permit from The City that declared plans to bulldoze the Pan home to make way for a high-speed rail that would carry millions of travelers North and South and provide thousands with decent jobs. Any protests of the Pan family displacement fell on deaf ears and with the

Pan home out of the way, the rail could bore through the dark side of Sunset Cliffs and tunnel the mystic depths of the great Pacific: all obstacles, surmountable. However, after the razing of the house, officials declared the Pan family missing—investigators say that one distant relation may know their whereabouts but is refusing to talk—and the railway project now stalled because Papa Pan was one of the vital project leaders and private donors; consequently, taxpayers are booing and hissing officials for proposing a spectacular railway that gave fat promises but has since been diverted by the histories, secrets, and fates of a seemingly ordinary family of six.

The Diner

by Tracy Shields

Carmela tasted the red on her lips. When she was nervous or excited she'd bite down, puncturing the skin and cause bleeding. She remembered hearing that the Egyptians used their own blood as make-up to lure potential lovers. But, when he entered the diner where she stood taking orders at the counter, holding a hand that was not hers, she wiped at her wounded lips, took their order, and skirted through the double doors to the kitchen. "It'll be alright, darling," George said to her from behind the line, "we'll spit in their soup." And as Carmela readied the bowls, she wondered how many drops of love would pass unnoticed in the Fasolada.

Subtle Hints

by Amy Simonson

She curls into a fetal position on the edge of the mattress, her back to his side of the bed. The bathroom door opens, and she fakes a snore as he slides beneath the covers. He scoots into her and his hand travels up her flanne-covered thigh, the hill-and-dale of her waist and up to her breasts, where five pearl buttons become kryptonite to his Superman-sized desire. The memory of last night, and the night before and the night before that deflate his passion. It's not worth it. He rolls over, his back to her side of the bed, and she breathes a sigh of relief.

Her Protectors

by Sondra Sula

They flanked her, breathing metallic, red-tinged flames from their lips onto her neck and down her bare shoulders. Wings sprouted from their strong, muscular golden backs like multicolored jewels. They were her protectors, and their fire sealed her from harm. She could only see them indirectly, at the very periphery of her vision. But she knew they were there. Always.

The Off Road

by Melody Gray

He dropped to his knees and kissed the ground he walked upon, and I wondered what he could possibly be so thankful for. He was one of the lost souls that wandered daily up and down that dingy street. Some twitching to their own obscure dance brought on by drugs not music, while others roamed, mumbling to themselves with a vacant stare in their eyes, lost in a place only they could understand. Girls showed up on that street corner young and innocent one day, but quickly became worn-out and tainted as they were eaten up by the drugs and predators that haunted them. Some days I could only stare straight ahead as I drove by, knowing those people were missed and loved by somebody. Knowing I was missing someone who was lost on a street just like that one while people stared and wondered where his family was.

Twist of Fate

by Nathalie Boisard-Beudin

Today I became a dandelion. Just like that, in a moment. I was standing at the bus stop when I suddenly felt my feet taking root and a surge of power coming up my body, making it explode in a flurry of green pointed leaves. My hair cut, often derided as feral and unkempt, took a turn for the worse and went semi-afro, also adopting a tint that had never been seen on a human head before – except for that of one Donna Summersault, drag queen at the GoGoClub in Vegas – and an amplitude that poked the eyes of the innocent bystanders around me. However, my ordeal wasn't finished and before I could protest – or try to at least, dandelions not being know for their vocal effects – my whole head turned into a fully deployed clock, exploding under the galling influence of a northern breeze to go forth and multiply. I resented this the most: I had never wanted any children.

Just Like Mom

by Carolyn Carceo

If I am lucky, I can look out the window early mornings, and see the little ones my age get on the big yellow thing, and leave, only to come back in the afternoon. Father says they are cursed, and must be educated to learn their place, so I must have nothing to do with them, or they will contaminate me; I am blessed, he says, because I know my place. Mother made sure I could cook and sew and do the other things females must know, including how to act toward a male--do as you're told, speak only when spoken to, and never raise your voice or argue. She did both one night when Father came to her, and she wasn't here the next morning. I had to burn her bed linen; it was all full of red liquid. Father says that soon he will teach me how to make a daughter, so that I may have a blessed one of my own to teach.

Becoming

by Sean Kennedy

From what I remember, it all began with an explosion of bright colours, splashing around me like raindrops of paint. The ground below me plunged beneath my feet, deep into an abyss of unknown mysteries and latent dreams. I began to rise, freeing myself from physical limitations, and took to the horizon like a ray of violet light. The images which filled my mind were fantastic; undiscovered worlds, far beyond the boundaries of human imagination, engulfed my vision and became part of my soul. I danced with the stars, falling in and out of time, and blasted my way through different realms of reality. It was at this moment I realized I was dead; but this knowledge held no significance since I now knew that death, in all its wonder, was only the beginning.

Trial by T-Shirt

by Scott Thouard

If only people would wear an announcement of their personalities as a slogan T-Shirt. The passive-aggressive type could bluster under the sternum-level text. I am full of strong beliefs and weak answers. Recently, at the Sushi corral, obliquely looking through an angled hygiene guard I faced clarity. There it was a shirt slogan. I hear voices... and they say they don't like you.

An Act of God

by Kerry Ashwin

It would be an act of God. I saw the body bobbing in the water, her head lolling to one side, the light on her jacket flashing, on, off, on, off, just to let me know she was still there. I could have tried, should have tried a little harder to save her, but when she slipped, it was I, not her, that saw my life flashing before my eyes. The things I could do, the places I could go... without her. I had planned this trip, the trip to end all trips, and now as she floats over the waves, taking her forever out to sea, her orange day-glow jacket dimming with the fading light, my own light gets stronger, brighter. Yes, it was all in the grand plan, His or mine, they will never know.

Part 6

The Last Time He Saw Her

by Nathan Tyree

Heller thinks that the last time he saw her face he didn't really look. It was just so familiar that he never needed to focus on the details, the lines around her eyes, the freckles on her cheek. There was no way that this would be the last time he saw her. Every day was still to come. The future, he thought, would stretch out forever. He was wrong.

A Righteous Dose

by Mark Rosenblum

The patient was lying on the hospital bed, his head completely bandaged due to injuries sustained in a car accident. He didn't speak English, so they called me -- the only bilingual doctor working the emergency room late shift. The patient began cursing in Spanish about not being able to see and complaining about the throbbing pain in his head. When I finished the initial medical consult, I ordered an injection of morphine. Later, after the patient died of an allergic reaction, I would be cleared of wrongdoing. I did not tell the investigation team I recognized the patient's voice or the tattoo on his neck, only that I clearly asked the patient to provide me with information on his medical allergies and the man who raped me said he had none.

Tarringtons

by Hosho McCreesh

I distinctly remember the day I learned the world was insane. I was 7 and standing in the living room of a tiny apartment, shaking hands with an old guy my Mom said was my 'only living grandfather.' He sat in his brown La-Z-Boy recliner, wearing an undershirt and skivvies, smoking and smoking Tarringtons as the grown-ups had grown-up talk. On the panel wall behind him hung two beautiful deer heads, each with deep, glassy-black eyes looking off at nothing. I stared and stared--breaking only occasionally to look at my grandfather, my mother as she held my little brother, then back to those eyes again. No one said a word about them... not a single goddamned word.

What Does Intervention Look Like?

by Caren Coté

Halfway across the span of the Golden Gate Bridge he saw her, a likely candidate, in the unmistakable pose of someone contemplating the jump. He pedaled slower as he neared her, casually watching sunlight glint off East Bay windows in the distance, the sense that the day was a special one building in his heart. He stopped to ask if she was all right; she laughed and pulled her auburn curls back from her face, tried to pass herself off as a tourist. "I can see my cousin's house from here," she said. He rode on, but stopped a few yards away. Before he had time to make necessary allowances for spontaneity, for this unbelievable stroke of luck, she vaulted over the rail in one smooth and practiced motion, like an Olympic gymnast, into the front of a school bus.

The Company Prison

by Suzanne Baran

Here I sit in corporate America feeling like Homer J. Simpson in sector R-8, cube 259A. That's me. I've been reduced to a number. Aren't we all, though? Is this how god classifies us, too, because there are too many people to keep track of and their petty wants and needs? I don't even know what I am supposed to be doing and I'm being watched.

Words to Hank

by Steven Kunert

Good men like you and me can't be kissing women when there's work to be done. We got wood to chop and pile, roof leaks to repair, beer to finish while cold wind dries sweat from our skin. The air smells of winter. So tell her, the hell with love, at least for a while. Good men don't waste time. We got a chimney to clean and some anti-freeze to put in the truck.

Longing

by Rachel Green

I watch from behind yellowed lace as she waves goodbye to her husband, a blown kiss caught and pressed to plum-painted lips. His car backs down the drive and merges with the tidal flow of traffic heading into the city. Why are so many cars silver these days? Is silver the new red for middle-aged men desperate to regain their virility? Ten minutes later her first trick of the day trots up the drive with a plastic Sainsbury's bag and a furtive expression. I hate her for being a prostitute while at the same time wishing I could afford her select rates.

Invisibility

by Kim Tairi

Layla's usually pale complexion was stained red with humiliation, she didn't want to be in the department store dressing room with her over-bearing mother hovering excitedly and popping her head in every few minutes to check on her. She was resigned to the inevitable horror that was to come when she went to school tomorrow, after months of wrapping her chest in bandages to hide her breasts, her mother had discovered her daily ritual and forced her to come on this stupid girly shopping excursion. The tears began as her mother's manicured hand with pale pink nail polish appeared over the top of the cubicle door with a dozen more bras, "Just try these ones on honey, they are sooo cute!" The worst thing was that Layla knew that she was about to lose her superpower... being invisible, it had taken her years to master. She breathed quietly, dressed in nondescript clothing and not one of her teachers or fellow students could remember her name. Instinctively she knew that everything was about to change, as she fumbled with the catch on the hideous contraption her mother handed her, she began to wonder how long it would take to develop another superpower, after all she was only ten.

Loopback

by Robert Clay

I've done it, I've finally figured out how to travel in time, well, nearly figured it out. Not into the future, that doesn't exist yet, but yes, into the past. And you don't need weird machines and lots of power and rotating wheels and stuff, just a certain way of thinking, just a thought powered way to get into that other time dimension that runs opposite to our time dimension, it's easy. I'm not going to bother you with the M Theory that permits this, none of you would understand anyway, and I've got better things to do you see, because there is a small problem, I don't quite know how to concentrate my thoughts into that quantum dimension yet. But I think I've solved it because all I need to do is that when I do figure it out, I'll go back in time and tell myself how to do it, so then I'll know and I can travel back and so on and so forth. All I have to do is wait and I don't care if the men in white coats peer at me through their pathetic little peep hole in my cell door, I'll deal with them later, I'll just keep waiting for myself here in this corner, forever if necessary.

The Undefeated

by Joseph Grant

While most of his friends and neighbors he grew up with were either in prison or in the ground, 20 year-old Ramon Mendoza had already slugged out a distinguished career in the ring. Undefeated, with a record of 38 and 0, with 2 draws, 5 TKO's and an impressive 31 knockouts, an all-time record at the old Olympic Stadium, Mendoza was something of an anomaly in the world of semi-professional boxing. Unusually tall and quick for a middleweight at 6'1" and with one of the longest reaches, his right was one of the best and most feared inside the ropes. On his way up, he had fought many strong and equally worthy contenders, just as he had pummeled many lesser opponents into tomorrow and he had paid his boxing dues and was a well-respected boxer. Coached early on at the fading First Street Gym in East L.A. by the legendary Armando "Pepe" Ruiz, a former middleweight champ who saw a spark of his former glory in the young Mendoza, immediately took him under his glove and put the kid on a strict regimen of diet, training and exercise to lose the baby fat, Mendoza's golden rise was much noticed and exploited by all of the fight magazines and pay-per-view bouts of the day. The early acclaim, money, constant late nights, women and drinks bought, however, brought into the ring a challenger he could neither control, train for or feint and his life began to become one prolonged standing 8 count after another until one day not long after Ruiz had finally given up on him, his last nameless trainer found him OD'd with the needle still stuck in his arm, the greatest contender of his generation brought down by the one opponent he could not beat.

I Can't Remember Her Name

by Jason Jordan

"How many people have you had sex with?" I asked her during a lull at work. Maybe we were flirting. She held up three fingers, and bowed her head in a coy, seductive fashion. When she asked me the same question, I formed a zero with my hand. She was sixteen and had slept with three men; I was eighteen and had slept with no women. I can't remember her name, but I do remember her blue eye shadow.

Carnivorous

by Erik Smetana

I am so hungry. Finnegan couldn't help but stare at the boy, watching him inhale the blue plate special fried chicken as though this were the boy's last meal or maybe the first in a very long time, but what surprised him more than the boy's appetite was his appearance, in one word dirty, but that didn't quite capture it all – greasy, tussled, filthy – but he kept this all to himself as he watched and wondered to himself how someone so young, so down on their luck had such perfect teeth: straight, snow white and gleaming – this irony was the very reason Finnegan offered to buy the boy a bite to eat when the boy approached him panhandling, although he tried to tell himself it was more than that. Teeth – dirty, disgusting things; food wedged between them (greasy chicken being one of the worst offenders); prone to discoloration; simply awful – when the youngest of the Pritchard boys, considered all of this he felt like smacking himself in the head as he wondered, *What possessed me to ever take up this profession?* As Jeannie's eyes opened, the only thing she could feel was cold, slowly she started to take in the shadowy surroundings, finally coming to realize she was strapped down – her wrists at least – in what appeared to be an old Morrison chair in need of grease on the hydraulics. Sturdy, solid, well-built; all were perfectly adequate ways to describe the selection of recliners, lounges, stools - chairs - that Jefferson had seen so far, but none possessed that certain something, the right lines, the panache he required for what would become the centerpiece of his art installation, so he kept on searching, waiting for inspiration to strike him. A dentist, a pudgy man hoping to look worldly, bought Jefferson Brown's "Dining Room for One;" the man hoped it would impress his new neighbor, a younger woman (an appraiser at one of the larger house's downtown) who until now had managed to evade his advances with claims of work, book club meetings and out of town guests - but the dentist knew better - he maintained his cool, waiting for the right moment to spur his gift on her, all the while knowing that if, when, she rejected him again there would be no choice but to resort to plan B because he couldn't afford another incident, another failure, like the one with the boy.

Ethereal Music, Eras Disjointed

by F. William Chickering

Driving to work this morning, I needed a break from my books-on-disc thriller's intensity. I found a wonderful bluegrass station, and listened happily for some miles. As the station began to fade during a Scruggs banjo lament for a lost girl, something magical occurred as strains of Vivaldi's baroque cello music began to provide backup to the energetic banjo and sad nasal voice. Then it was the warm, rich cello with a bright harpsichord continuo layered atop the distinctive banjo and sad lyrics. Back and forth they went, long past over recent past and back again, providing musical and historical counterpoint, causing me to wonder if the banjo were really the New World answer to the harpsichord's light, twangy tone. CDs and iPods fail miserably at the gift of serendipity that the radio, an archaic reminder of my childhood, still provides as a lagniappe from time to lucky time.

Tag

by Li-Ann Wong

He didn't know she knew he was waiting for her at the school gates, waiting till she was away on her bicycle before tailing behind, playing an increasingly not-so-subtle game of bicycle tag. By the time they whizzed past the fifth bend, they could no longer pretend that one did not know what the other was doing. She pedaled as hard as she could down the next alleyway to widen the chasm between them, knowing that this meant she would have to make a drastic detour. But so be it. At last she arrived, biting her lip as she slammed the brakes and slid off the seat, breaths coming in short puffs, relief tinged with disappointment as she chucked her bike on the ground. He was a sweetiepie, but he could never see this rundown ramshackle of a house she called home.

In Flagrant Communication

by Peter Cherches

When I was a child I walked into my parents' bedroom and caught them on the telephone. Actually, I caught them on telephones. You see, they each had their own extension and they were having an exchange with an unknown third party--though there could have been more. After all, if my folks had two phones who knows how many parties there could have been on the other end. Though I only heard my parents' portion of the conversation, it seemed rather uneventful, at least as far as I can remember, these many years later. I guess it was a conference call, but I was too young to understand that.

A Series

by Christine Hamm

My grandmother's gray kitten balanced like a handful of feathers on my shoulder, his nose deep in my ear, when I crayoned the telephone book. The zig-zag scar on my thigh is from a tabby who used me as a launching pad when pursued by my cousin. In Harlem, I wooed a stray with a split nose by leaving open cans of Nine Lives on the fire escape; he thanked me by crapping in my flower-box. I got my first pet-store Persian when I got my first apartment, a voiceless black and white who offered her big, soft belly to anyone with warm hands. My boyfriend named his fat calico after an ex, so I renamed her after a racecar driver and trained her to spit up in his shoes. Last week when it rained, a pregnant cat dragged by my basement window, her tail as tall and rigid as any fist.

Rani

by Fiona Rebeiro

It's 3.17am on a Tuesday and she's pacing the kitchen, seemingly unaware of the interruption she's causing to my sleep. It's been twenty-seven months sharing a shoebox of an apartment and yet she remains the ultimate mystery. A lady of the night, she has never once shown any type of gratitude toward me for opening up my home, my heart and my fridge. I saved her from a life on the streets, from a bleak future and a dysfunctional family, yet she treats me as if I am nothing more than an obstacle in her quest for 16-hour sleeping sessions and nighttime exploits. I throw back the covers, step barefoot onto the cold tiles of the kitchen and find her walking in circles next to the back entrance. I turn the key, open the screen door and watch her move steadily into the courtyard, the grey hairs of her tail shining in the moonlight.

Chomsky, I Love You Dearly

by Tim Horvath

A sentence is a grammatical entity of a somewhat arbitrary nature; for instance, recall that teacher that stood there and proclaimed stone-facedly that a sentence contains a single, um, idea. Harrumph! Take this book and prop it like a spade in a clump of d irt and look around now—how many "sentences" do you see before you? Let the teeming, hydra-headed moment enter you like the day's first cigarette; inhale its geometries and its textures; let it titillate your rods and cones like an exotic dancer, this particular dollop of space-time, meeting point of objective world and your subjectivity and, oddly enough, mine. Now, if you are not too timid, not too cowed by rules inculcated in you when you were too young to reflect on them, not too taken with the illusions of completeness and authority and even immortality, in short not too chickenshit to write in a book, then cull one sentence from the innumerable possibilities offered up by the scene before you (and don't forget what isn't there—the inverted cow, the spiral-galaxy of luminescent plankton, the world's third-largest spatula, the love that left you), and write it out in painstaking longhand. Here: _____
_____.

Die and Let Live

by Madam Z

No one is as important as he thinks he is. We all think, even if we don't admit it, that our death will leave a huge hole in the fabric of our family, of society, the world, maybe even the universe, but it won't, guys. Sorry to disappoint you, but we're all expendable; even your closest family and friends will eventually mend that hole in the fabric and go on with their lives. Sure, a few people will shed a few tears, and if you're rich and famous your name will be in the newspaper for a day or two, but then, like a puff of smoke on a windy day, you'll disappear, and two or three years later, they'll be playing "Dead or Alive?" with your name as one of the questions. We're all just a collection of atoms, held together in temporary cohesion, waiting to be scattered and then reassembled in various other forms, maybe part of carrot and/or a cricket, maybe a canoe or some Coca-Cola. I kind of like that idea for my own ultimate fate, because, you see, I am actually very important, because I may become part of a fine canoe when I die, but it would be even better if some of my atoms ended up in a can of Coca-Cola, because everyone knows that things go better with Coke.

X

by Chi Sherman

I wanted to fall in love with you so that I could stop looking, could stop hoping, could finally stop wondering if the woman I was destined to spend the rest of my life with had been the delivery driver climbing into her truck outside my apartment building; the middle manager who had interviewed me for a corporate job; or the drugstore clerk who had rung up my tampons. The plan was to suspend ourselves comfortably between bliss and domesticity, balancing the mundane reality of grocery store trips and oil changes with hushed personal phone calls from our cubicles at work and romantic weekend getaways. Our love would creep in like fall putting on her colors and I would find myself thinking about you more and more, remembering the first time you came to my apartment and stopped at the grocery to buy me flowers, suspending myself in the memory of your hands in the darkness of my bedroom, your voice low and urgent in my ear, all the while a dusting of pink rising above my collar. I wanted to save I love you for a nondescript morning when we would wake, hazy and thick with sleep, and I would tangle our feet together, give you my hip and morning scent, my languid laziness, and say so softly the words that would signal a crescendo into marriage, homes, children, all I had been promised since I had draped a towel over my head as a child and walked down a pretend aisle. The reality of love encircled us but drove on like cars navigating a roundabout; we stopped talking and I started going to bed angry as I lost my grip on words like *forever* and *finally*. After we broke, there was a chance at reconciliation and I found myself wanting to try harder to fall in love with you, but as I opened my mouth to say yes to anything you asked, I heard my mother's voice say I already had plans for Friday night.

Roommates

by Naomi Garnice

The last year has taken so many I-love-yous from me. I whispered each one slow and honest, like I was covering them in foil; like I'd make us last. I gave them all to you one after another like candy, and you always tried to say it back the same way. The apartment for rent next to ours looks how this one did the day they gave us the keys. I stared through the Phoenician blinds because I wanted that first day back. I pressed my nose to the glass and all I saw was an empty tin heart.

A Bit of Stupid Nonfiction

by Claire Zulkey

We were in Sorrento and had gone out for dinner and drinks, but not before I took some Italian-labeled cold medicine. I could tell something was wrong on the way home from the bar and I had to kick a party out of our hotel room because I felt so awful. I was forced to sleep in an upper bunk and realized, when it was time to throw up, that I could either jump down and possibly barf upon landing, or be sick in my shirt and then climb down; I chose the latter. I threw my clothes on the patio, took a shower, gulped down two glasses of water sitting on the sink and crawled back up the ladder to bed. The next morning I felt better but then I heard my friend Emily say "Y'all, I can't find my contact lenses!" Our friend Iona asked where she put them and Emily told us she couldn't find her case so filled two glasses with saline solution and used those instead.

Mumbai

by Nicole Taylor

The girl makes the pavement outside Leopold's her playground. During the afternoon she fashions daisy-chains from flowers stolen from the Cross Maidan, draping them over tourists milling about the Gateway of India in exchange for a rupee or two. Of an evening, she is a regular fixture outside the restaurant, skinny brown legs dangling over the side of the gutter, a small grimy face illuminated by the light fixtures. She wears a flimsy cotton dress and is barefoot in the approaching winter. A white woman with scented, golden hair comes out of Leopold's onto the street. The girl springs up to the woman and asks in a quiet but proud voice, "One rupee, Madam?"

Untitled

by Jeremy Blachman

"I know what you do with Tylenol," she said as she dropped the capsule in a cup of hot water and stirred it around with a fork. "How old am I... am I dead... is this my house?" she asked. The phone rang less and less these days, and even when it did, she didn't always know how to answer it. *Did I eat dinner?* she wondered, even as the half-empty plate sat in front of her. "Will I get better?" she asked, when she could remember enough to know something was wrong ~ and even asking the question was considered a triumph, as triumphs got smaller and smaller. I am losing my grandma.

Singularity

by Doug Wacker

Despite all of the planning and programming, the hours upon hours of research and discussion, the combined intelligence of thousands of scientists, philosophers, and engineers, fate dictated that this radical change, this irrevocable alteration of the human order, would be initiated by a mistake, by a cleaning robot of all things. Its brand name was Abberdon, after an ancient god of war, which still symbolized strength and tenacity in the modern psyche. ?Let Abberdon Defeat Your Dirt!? was the motto. As this particular unit wound around a corner in the Middleton Country Club, it glimpsed a flash of its reflection on a recently polished serving tray. Perhaps a circuit blew at this precise moment, or some wires got crossed, maybe the unit?s recognition of a yet to be eradicated dust bunny resulted in a divine catharsis? Regardless, at 05:39 on February 15th 2035, this state-of-the-art, highly efficient RL74, commonly known as the Abberdon Cleaning Robot, recognized itself as a sentient being.

New Mom

by Amy Sue Nathan

I wheeled my newborn son around the mall in his top-of-the-line stroller, the same way I carried car keys at 16 – proud and careful, making sure everyone heard me silently screaming my new identity. The buggy was laden with the best in baby supplies and extras of everything (just in case), yet nary a shopping bag. I was surprised at the number of people perusing the mall that mid-winter Tuesday morning -- mothers chasing toddlers, sale shoppers scurrying, men and women grabbing lattes; a hairy man talking to himself by the fountain, teenagers home from school flirting with one another but pretending not to and bored shoe salesmen eating Nathan's hot dogs for breakfast. My son slept unaware, yet I was overwhelmed – not at the wonder or the newness, the two-for-one sweaters or even the hot dogs for breakfast – but that so many people were breathing on my baby. I retraced my personal path around the perimeter of the mall, bundled us up and headed out into the cold, half-filled parking lot where I repacked the supplies and stroller into the hatchback. Would I ever shop again?

Addition

by Paul Sullivan

The dogs and I crowded around my wife. She relieved herself as if she had privacy. One line bad, two lines dad, was how I read the box. The older Lab, a retired breeder of guide dogs, sighed and flopped to the tile floor as if to say, what's the big deal? The puppy started wiggling and sniffed at the stick. I was at the back of the pack, but I could see enough to count the lines: we would soon be five.

The Invisible Six

by Robert McEvily

Bonus Section!

*Four Sixes
by Six-Year-Old
David Wain!*

Soup Can

by six-year-old David Wain

Once there was this lady who lost a soup can. She called, "Help!" Just then someone came. "Can I help you?" He found it somehow. They were both happy, and she made soup.

The Dog Who Saw a Big Hog

by six-year-old David Wain

There once was a dog. He saw a big hog. Then he saw some fog. He started to jog. He jogged to a log. And there he got killed.

The Elephish

by six-year-old David Wain

Once there was an Elephish. His Mom was an elephant and his Dad was a fish. This Elephish went to the smore. In it he saw some lore. In the lore he saw more and more. He ate the lore and he was dead.

The Dog Who Would Always Fly

by six-year-old David Wain

Once there was a dog who would always fly. He had 200 wings and was rich. One day he was flying in the sky and saw an airplane. He was out of control. Then he flew away. He was safe.

About the Authors

Kerry Ashwin has a healthy ego, a fertile imagination and a robust work ethic. On any given day, she can be heard to say, "Oh, for heavens sake!"

Nicole Andrea Aube was born in Levis, Quebec on November 25, 1980. She became a member of the Royal Academy of Dance in England in her teens, and holds a University degree in English and Music from Toronto's York University. In 2004, two of her books were published, *Waterbird* (stories, Gutter Press Toronto) and *The Red Lantern* (poems, Widows and Orphans, Kitchener).

austere seeker lives, works, and writes in Mumbai.

Julian Baker started writing one weekend in June, and thinks he would like to write more.

Suzanne Baran, a former content writer/programmer for Yahoo's front page, is now an executive content producer at Celebuzz.com. She also reviews music & films for *The Big Takeover*.

David Barringer is an author, freelance writer, graphic designer, photographer, and artist. He grew up in Michigan. He now lives with his family in North Carolina.

Diane Becker is a writer and artist who sometimes finds herself in dark places, but never forgets to pick up the milk.

Lauren Becker has stories in or forthcoming in *Word Riot*, *Dogzplot*, *Wigleaf*, and *Mud Luscious*. She is quite clumsy and prefers whisky to tequila.

Jeremy Blachman went to Harvard Law School, started writing a blog, got a book deal, wrote a novel (*Anonymous Lawyer*, published by Henry Holt & Co.), and is now trying to make things work as a writer.

Nathalie Boisard-Beudin is French. She lives in Italy. Anything else you think you might need to know about her, you'll have to invent.

Ryan W. Bradley is currently working on his MFA in creative writing from Pacific University. His poetry and fiction have appeared in *The Oregonian*, *A Thousand Faces*, *Third Wednesday*, *Yippee Magazine*, and *Gander Press Review*. He lives in Southern Oregon with his wife and two sons.

Diane Brady is a Peace Corps Volunteer serving in Belize, C.A.

Paul D. Brazill lives and writes in Bydgoszcz, Poland.

Quin Browne is pretty content with her life. She dedicates the work contained in this volume to Neal. It's not her best work, but, it'll do.

Georgina Bruce feels guilty when she does anything other than writing. She writes short stories and wants readers.

Christen Buckler is a creative writing major at Florida State University. If she can't make a million dollars with her writing by the time she graduates, she is going to become a high school English teacher.

Kathryn Burkett writes poems, makes collages and altered books, and eats donuts in Central Florida with her wonderful husband and two amazing Dachshunds.

Salvatore Buttaci is an obsessive-compulsive writer from Princeton, West Virginia. Enough said.

Alice J. Byrd is 15 years old and lives in Wasilla, Alaska. She's on a journey to figure out this thing called life.

Elissa Cain spends her time working, while her mind wanders to things of loftier heights. *(Just don't tell her boss.)*

Carolyn Carceo lives on Massachusetts' North Shore and works in Boston. She's the oldest of four, and a mom to two catkids.

Jeanette Cheezum, a charter member of the Hampton Roads Writers, has been published in *Smith Magazine's Six-Word Memoirs*, *Gather*, *Pen Pricks*, *The Verb*, and *Verbsap*.

Peter Cherches is the author of two volumes of short prose: *Condensed Book* and *Between a Dream and a Cup of Coffee*, as well as several limited-edition art books.

F. William Chickering spends his time surrounded by hundreds of thousands of books, but only gets to read microfiction (and picture books to his three wonderful children).

Robert Clay is a Seafarer now stranded on land. He lives in Cornwall in the UK.

Christopher Cocca's short fiction, nonfiction, and poetry have appeared in *Elimae*, *Thieves Jargon*, *Boston Literary Magazine*, *Geez Magazine*, *Brevity*, *The Ooze*, *The Lantern*, and other venues. He is a graduate of Yale Divinity School.

Caren Coté enjoys people-watching in and around Portland, Oregon.

Linda Courtland lives and writes in Los Angeles. Her stories have recently appeared in *Momaya Press's 2008 Annual Review*, *The Binnacle's Annual Ultra-Short Competition Edition*, *Shroud Magazine*, and an anthology of short fiction entitled *People of Few Words*.

Craig Daniels is sure it was hiding in plain site, and when he came upon it, he knew it was always there waiting for him.

Stephen J. Davis is an elementary school teacher near San Francisco, California. He lives with his wife, daughter, and two cats.

Rayne Debski lives in central Pennsylvania. Her work has appeared or is forthcoming in *Rose & Thorn Ezine*, *Thema*, *REAL*, and *XX Eccentric: 2009 Main Street Rag Short Fiction Anthology*. Her work has also been selected for dramatic readings by theater groups in New York and Pennsylvania.

Tess Dickenson is just a normal Southern girl who started writing when she was 10 and hasn't stopped. She and her family bask in the sunshine of their Arizona home.

Rod Drake grew up in the Midwest, but currently resides, works and writes in Las Vegas, Nevada. He's been a technical writer and an editorial compliance officer, but he enjoys writing short fiction best. For a laugh, he likes to stand convention on its head, and thinks coincidence makes interesting fiction.

Steve Edgehouse is from Dun Glen, Ohio, and teaches writing at Bowling Green State University.

Emily Anne Epstein is a writer/photographer/editor based in Buenos Aires.

Sian Evans is currently undertaking a BA HONS degree in English Literature and Creative Writing at The University of Salford in Greater Manchester.

Thom Gabrukiewicz is fiercely loyal, a work in progress, a hopeless romantic, a realist, kind, big-hearted, and sometimes an asshole.

Timothy Gager is the author of seven books of short fiction and poetry. He hosts the Dire Literary Series in Cambridge, Massachusetts every month and is the co-founder of the Somerville News Writers Festival.

Brenda J. Gannam is an Arab-American poet, writer, and visual artist who hails from Georgia and has lived in Brooklyn, New York for the past 28 years.

Naomi Garnice is the author of many other stories only slightly longer than "Roommates."

Brad Gayman, a graduate of the New School for General Studies, is a former high school math teacher. He currently lives in Manhattan and enjoys trivia.

Mel George lives in Oxford, UK, and writes a bit for work and mostly for pleasure. She's had short pieces published at *Every Day Fiction*, and edits the online Brit-lit magazine *The Pygmy Giant*.

David Gianatasio's *Mind Games* was published last October by Word Riot Press. He is also the author of *Swift Kicks*, published in 2007 by So New Publishing.

Joseph Grant is originally from New York City and currently resides in Los Angeles. His work has appeared in countless literary journals and e-zines, such as *Byline, New Authors Journal, Howling Moon Press, Hack Writers, New Online Review, Indite Circle,* and *Cerebral Catalyst.* He is far and away 6S's most prolific writer.

Eugenia E. Gratto is not from Iowa. She's not from California, either, but she lives there now, where she commits tiny acts of fiction and nonfiction on her blog.

Melody Gray lives in British Columbia, Canada. She spends most of her time reading, writing, and in her garden.

Rachel Green is a writer from the Hills of Derbyshire in England. She lives with her two female partners, their three kids and their three dogs, and only occasionally gets them all mixed up. She is plagued by demons who want her advice about towels.

Jasmin Guleria is a freelance writer currently residing in New York.

Amy Guth is the founder of Pilcrow Lit Fest and the author of *Three Fallen Women* (So New Media Publishing, 2006). She has written for *The Believer, Monkeybicycle, Ninth Letter, Four Magazine,* and *Bookslut,* among others.

Christine Hamm is working towards her PhD in English Literature. Her poetry has been published in many journals, including *The Adirondack Review, Pebble Lake Review, Lodestar Quarterly, Poetry Midwest, MiPoesias, Rattle, Blue Fifth Review, Horseless Review, Snow Monkey*, and *Exquisite Corpse*. She has been nominated twice for a Pushcart Prize.

Paige L. Hanson, a twenty-something running amok in the not-so-quiet suburbs of Detroit, will likely be killed by avalanche of comic books.

Zeptimius Hedrapor lives in Amsterdam and writes short stories sporadically as a hobby.

Bob Heman's prose poems and other small prose pieces have appeared in *Sentence, Quick Fiction, Paragraph, First Intensity*, and *The Prose Poem: An International Journal*, and online at *Mad Hatters' Review* and *Tuesday Shorts*.

Sean Patrick Hill earned his MA in Writing from Portland State University, where he won the Burnam Graduate Award. His poems appear or are forthcoming in *Exquisite Corpse, elimae, diode, In Posse Review, Willow Springs, RealPoetik, New York Quarterly, Sawbuck*, and *Quarter After Eight*.

Peter Holm-Jensen lives in a rainy medieval town in the UK.

David Holzel's local paper is *The Washington Post*, which has a new policy of canceling your subscription before you have a chance to cancel it.

Tim Horvath is the author of *Circulation*, recently released by sunnyoutside press. His writing appears in *Alimentum: The Literature of Food*, *Web Conjunctions*, *Puerto del Sol*, and many other journals. He has received a Yaddo residency, and is currently the author of the world's longest six-sentence story, "Luminous Specificity," which was featured in *Six Sentences, Volume 1*. Tim teaches fiction writing at Chester College of New England.

Natalie Jabbar wants to tell you *so* many stories.

Prachi Jain writes short fiction, essays, and children's stories.

Rebecca Jane is a novelist and freelance writer based in San Diego. She is trained in English and Chinese literature and writes in both languages.

Keturah Jones somehow fell into teaching English, and now absolutely adores it. She has two gorgeous girls (one born in Australia and the other in Taiwan), and a handsome WWII History buff as a husband. *(Oh, and her students are all very cool, too!)*

Jason Jordan is a writer from New Albany, Indiana, who always says he's from Louisville, Kentucky, because people actually know where that is. His fiction has appeared or is forthcoming in *Beeswax Magazine*, *Hobart*, *Keyhole Magazine*, *Monkeybicycle*, *Pindeldyboz*, *Storyglossia*, *Word Riot*, and many other publications. Jordan is also Editor-in-Chief of the literary magazine *decomP*.

Sean Kennedy attends the University of Salford in Manchester, England.

Lakin Khan lives and writes in and around Northern California.

Michael J. Killips is trying to get the words unstuck from his head and down on paper.

Donna Kirk is a good friend of Tim Horvath, which makes her cool with the 6S crowd.

Eric Kramer is a sophomore at Armstrong Atlantic State University in Savannah, Georgia, majoring in English.

Steven Kunert has published prose and poetry stretching back for 30 years in publications such as *The Starving Artist Times*, *Dude*, *Rio Grande Review*, *The Oregonian*, and more recently in *Word Riot*, *decomP*, *American Satellite Magazine* and *Poetry Superhighway*. He teaches in the English Department at Oregon State University in Corvallis, where he lives.

Neil LaBute is a playwright, screenwriter, and film director. His latest play, *reasons to be pretty*, just opened on Broadway.

Tara Lazar loves trying to compose witty bios that make her sound interesting, but often fails. Her short fiction has appeared in *Six Sentences Volume 1*, *Boston Literary Magazine* and *flashquake*. (Hard to believe she also writes children's books, huh?)

Heather Leet is a modern day Robin Hood, but instead of stealing from the rich she cajoles them into giving her money to help fund programs that will hopefully one day make the world a better place.

Tao Lin is a poet, novelist and short story writer. *Eeeee Eee Eeee*, his debut novel, was published in 2007. His forthcoming books include a novella, *Shoplifting from American Apparel*, to be published in September 2009, and his second novel, *Richard Yates*, to be published early in 2010.

Joe Lo Truglio, who was born in New York, grew up in Florida, and now lives in California, is an actor, comedian, producer and screenwriter. His credits as an actor include appearances in *Superbad*, *Hitch*, *The Ten*, *The Baxter*, *Pineapple Express*, *The Station Agent*, *Reno 911!: Miami*, and most recently, *I Love You, Man*. (And make sure you catch him as Billy in My Damn Channel's *Horrible People*.)

Jodi MacArthur, currently exiled in deep southern Texas, is a Seattle author hoping to write her way back to the Pacific Northwest. In her spare time, she twitters at her beloved finches, Edgar and Emily, and drinks coffee - but never at the same time.

Ravi Mangla lives in Fairport, NY. His short fiction has recently appeared online at *Hobart*, *Pindeldyboz*, *Sleepingfish*, *elimae*, *McSweeney's Internet Tendency*, and is forthcoming in print in *One World: A Global Anthology of Short Stories* (New Internationalist).

Donna Martines is a graphic designer who dabbles in writing and most things artsy.

Doug Mathewson favors hats, and rarely turns down dessert. His work most recently has appeared in *The Boston Literary Magazine*, *Cezanne's Carrot*, *Gloom Cupboard*, *Poor Mojo's Almanac(k)*, *Tuesday Shorts*, and *55 Words*.

Hosho McCreesh writes, paints, works, & lives in the desert Southwest ~ only 3 of which he likes. He loves black cherry chutney & has seen a few deer up close.

Robert McEvily is the creator and editor of *Six Sentences*. He lives in New York City with his lovely girlfriend Jill.

Peggy McFarland, winner of the January 2009 "Six of the Month" Award (for "New Day"), lives in New Hampshire with her family, and tends bar for a living.

Doug McIntire is a central Texas author whose work has appeared in *The Tiny Globule*, *The Dunesteef Audio Fiction Magazine* (as a podcast), *The Abacot Journal*, *SNM Horror Magazine*, *The Monsters Next Door* and the NVF 2008 Halloween anthology, *And Soon... The Darkness*. He rides a motorcycle and likes to spend time with his wife and two children.

Kevin Michaels, a writer and surfer who lives on the Jersey Shore, is everything New Jersey (attitude, edginess, Bruce Springsteen... but not Bon Jovi). His work has been featured in *Word Riot*, *The Literary Review*, *Darkest Before the Dawn*, and *Dogzplot*.

Lisa Miller lives in Washington on a Christmas tree farm in the hills, and loves to Google old addresses when she's not busy working, walking her dogs, or keeping track of her family.

Megan Monserez is currently a Ph.D. candidate at the University of Maryland, College Park.

Rick Moody's novels include *Garden State*, *The Ice Storm*, and *The Diviners*. He is also a musician and a composer.

Susan Moody is blessed with a huge circle of friends and family that seem to be entertained by her stories. (At least that's what they tell her.)

Mindy Munro is a sporadic blogger.

Amy Sue Nathan is a writer, editor, blogger, and single mother attempting to thrive in a small (and very married) Midwestern suburb.

Alyssa Ning is a college girl attempting to find the right words.

Valerie O'Riordan's stories can be found online at *Wufniks*, *The Pygmy Giant*, *Pequin*, *For Every Year*, and *Dogmatika*.

Jillian Parker is a mom to five children, an autism activist, and a Russian/English translator. She recently relocated from chilly Alaska to foggy Northern California.

Whitney Pastorek is a senior writer at *Entertainment Weekly*, and a native Texan. Credits include *The New York Times*, *Sports Illustrated*, *The Village Voice*, *NPR's Morning Edition*, and the recent essay collection *Rock and Roll Cage Match (Whitney vs. Mariah, Whitney wins)*. She is unapologetically based out of Los Angeles.

Jessica Patient, winner of the 2008 Worldskills UK Creative Writing Competition, lives in Bedfordshire, England.

Pamila Payne writes small stories about herself and long novels about the *Bella Vista Motel*.

Juliana Perry is a single mom of three, a lover of all things wine, cheese and bread, a maintainer of all things house and home, a student of business and psychology, and a professional scheduler and multi-tasker.

Absolutely*Kate *(Kate Pilarcik of RiverView Studios)* is an ardent lover of words and their play and their say and will string 'em along the way pearls of wisdom and rubies of relevant thought should be most charmingly necklaced.

Sherrie Pilkington is a forty-something writer who is most comfortable with nonfiction. She enjoys funny snippets of fiction, and dreams of creating prose that feeds the soul.

Arsalan Pirzada wishes people spoke music.

Alyssa Quintieri is a California dreamer living in New Jersey.

Fiona Rebeiro strings words together to create sentences to fill the blank pages magazines can't sell to advertisers. Her work has appeared in *Yen*, *Flux*, *Nylon*, *Soma*, *Coolhunting*, *The Age*, *Beat*, and *Pulp*.

Timothy P. Remp lives in New Hampshire with his family and *Dr. Who* collection. He looks forward to showing his father-in-law a western.

Allan Revich is a Canadian artist and writer living in Toronto. His work has appeared in numerous small press publications, in international exhibitions, and on many websites. He is active in the international Fluxus and mail art communities.

Lisa Reynolds is a mom of three and grandma to one living temporarily in Eastern Oregon. She goes to school full time and works for a major hotel chain. Besides writing, she enjoys spending as much time as she can with her family.

Shelly Rae Rich likes to make things up and mix them with truth. Her fiction is found or forthcoming in print and online publications including *Apalachee Review*, *Duck and Herring's Pocket Field Guide*, *Opium Magazine*, *elimae*, *Scapegoat Review*, *Moon Drenched Fables*, *Right Hand Pointing*, *Ghoti*, *Juked*, *Ducts*, *Eyeshot*, and *VerbSap*, and has been translated into two languages. Shelly co-edits the micro-fiction ezine *Tuesday Shorts*.

Ryan Ridge hails from Louisville, Kentucky (the birthplace of the high-five). He is currently an MFA student and Creative Writing instructor at University of California, Irvine. His work has appeared in *5_Trope*, *Chunklet*, *Salt Hill*, *Yankee Pot Roast*, and elsewhere on the Web and in print. His story "Tomahawk Cuts Rain" was nominated for the 2008 Million Writers Award.

Chris Roberts was nominated for The Pushcart Prize in 2003. His work has been published in *The Powhattan Review*, *The London Magazine*, and his essay on *The New Yorker* can be found on the *3:AM Magazine* website, non-fiction. He lives in Brooklyn, New York.

Benjamin Robinson is otherwise disposed.

Ian Rochford, a screenwriter, recently rediscovered the pleasures of writing short stories. He lives in Australia.

Mark Rosenblum is a New York native who now lives in Southern California. His work has been featured in *Tiferet*, *Thirteen Magazine*, *Boston Literary Magazine*, *AlienSkin Magazine*, *Insolent Rudder*, and *Everyday Fiction*. He was awarded Honorable Mention in the 2006 Mindprints Flash Fiction Contest.

Nicole Roura fancies writing in her jammies, and only in just the right kinda light.

Patrick Salmon studied writing at the University of Washington.

Harry B. Sanderford is a Central Florida surfing cowboy who'd sooner spin yarns than mend fences.

Oceana Setaysha is a 17-year-old girl who has just finished high school and wants to see the world. She considers herself an artist, writer, poet, and musician. She used to listen to people who told her to be realistic, but she doesn't anymore, because she came to her senses and realized there's no point.

Lee Shafer lives in Redondo Beach with her husband and two boys. In her free time, she writes and designs jewelry.

Emily Sheer is a high school senior who spends a fair amount of time reading and writing. Her friends know her for her abstract personality and robot drawings. She's also an avid blogger.

Chi Sherman is an Indianapolis-based writer who has authored and self-published three chapbooks of poetry and creative nonfiction (*amative*, *beneath this skin*, and *mosaic*), as well as a spoken-word CD (*wild / tendril*).

Tracy Shields graduated from Rutgers University, magna cum laude, with a degree in English Literature and Journalism. She was Concept Editor of *Painted Bride Quarterly* from 2001-2007. She currently works and writes from home in New Jersey, and has two beautiful sons, Daniel and Julien.

Tovli Simiryan lives in West Virginia with her husband, Yosif.

Linda Simoni-Wastila, by day, is a proper academic – a "publish or perish" type who resides in tall towers with the likes of Rapunzul. Evenings, she morphs into a lovable mom and wife, plays with her children, hangs with the hubby. When darkness falls, when the house stills... she writes.

Amy Simonson is a wife, mother, and former Labor and Delivery nurse. She writes from northeast Ohio, and her short story, "Third Shift," was published in the 2008 anthology *Workers Write! Tales from the Clinic* (Blue Cubicle Press). She's currently slogging through the third draft of her second novel.

James Simpson is a freelance journalist and award-winning fiction writer. He is currently hip deep in his first novel and hopes to be up to his neck in it before long.

Erik Smetana's work can be found in *52nd City*, *Boston Literary Magazine*, *Thieves Jargon*, *The Late Late Show* and *The Birmingham Arts Journal*. He is currently enrolled in graduate studies for creative writing at Lindenwood University (just outside of St. Louis).

Hailey Sowden, a high school student in Texas, is unusually bad at writing bios.

Ben Spivey's writing has appeared or is forthcoming in *Titular Journal, No Posit, Robot Melon,* and *Abaculus II* (published by Leucrota Press). He lives in Atlanta, Georgia.

Brian Steel is a writer and poet living in Baltimore, Maryland. He takes most of his short story topics from experiences had several years ago while driving Route 66. (Good name for a road.)

L. Allison Stein remains small in stature, but big in heart.

Daniel Stine is an ex-pat American. He currently resides in south China, Guangdong province, high up in the Pearl River Delta, where he teaches English with his wife in their own private school. Daniel is a life long writer and lover of words. He is presently working on a book of poetry (*Drops of Lucidity*) and a sci-fi novel.

Belinda Subraman is a poet, writer and artist currently living in Ruidoso, New Mexico. Her writing can be found in over 400 journals, reviews, anthologies, ezines, books and chapbooks, including *Puerto del Sol, Main Street Rag, Big Bridge, mgversion2, Electica, Best Texas Writing 2, Out of Line,* and *Unlikely Stories*.

Sondra Sula is an artist and writer who loves solitude, flowers, and creativity of all kinds. She lives in a house in Aurora, Illinois filled with art, bones, curiosities and dog hair.

Paul Sullivan writes the *Wealth Matters* column for *The New York Times*. He has written about issues concerning the wealthy – from private banking and wealth management to philanthropy and inheritance battles – for many years. In addition to *The Times*, his stories have appeared in *Conde Nast Portfolio*, *The International Herald Tribune*, *Barron's* and *The Financial Times*, where he was that paper's first dedicated reporter covering high-net-worth investors.

Libby Sumner lives with her husband and a small zoo of animals (including but not limited to horses and tarantulas) in Alabama where she continues to work on her novel-in-progress, *Murder Gone South*.

Kelley A. Swan hasn't met Stephen King, which is very unfair. Her uncle had him as a teacher.

Kim Tairi has two daughters, and a day job as a librarian in Melbourne, Australia. She often wishes she had a superpower, and the ability to time travel.

Steve Talbert is a proud son of Shelbyville, Indiana. He enjoys writing about his hometown and its people, and has published several articles about both in the town's local newspaper.

Christine Taylor is a California writer, artist, and social media consultant who loves mystery and adventure, is convinced dreams come true, and considers it her mission in life to help others realize that fact.

Nicole Taylor is an Australian based writer. She edits the literary biannual *Sketch*.

Scott Thouard is an Australian writer of the short form.

Tammi J. Truax is a freelance writer, community activist, and single mom.

Paige Turner writes for a living and is infatuated with her pen name.

Nathan Tyree's work has appeared in *Flesh and Blood, Doorknobs and Body Paint, The Flash, Bare Bone, Dogmatika, Wretched and Violent,* and *The Empty Page: Stories Inspired by the Songs of Sonic Youth.*

Doug Wacker is a research fellow at the University of Edinburgh. He lives with his lovely wife, Kim, rambunctious toddler, Eilidh, and two persnickety cats, Luna and Nimbus.

David Wain is a comedian, writer, actor and director. He is also a co-founding member of the comedy trio *Stella*, and recently directed and co-wrote *Role Models*, starring Paul Rudd and Seann William Scott. (*Aisle Six*, David's aptly named 1991 NYU student film, was screened at Sundance and won numerous awards on the festival circuit.)

Sarah Wallis recently completed an MA at UEA Norwich England in Poetry, and is now studying for an M.Phil. at Birmingham U. (She hopes to put off stepping back into the real world for a while.)

Bruce Weber is the author of four books of poetry: *These Poems are Not Pretty*, *How the Poem Died*, *Poetic Justice*, and *The First Time I Sex with T S Eliot*. By day, he is the Senior Curator of 19th Century Art at the National Academy Museum.

Caroline Wells is a mother of two who's been married for 33 years.

Maggie Whitehead is interested in things that are interesting. Her favorite TV shows are *LOST*, *Survivor*, *The Amazing Race*, *The Wire*, *Flight of the Conchords*, and *Project Runway*.

Adam J. Whitlatch is the author of the novels *The Blood Raven: Retribution* and *E.R.A. - Earth Realm Army*. He lives with his wife, Jessica, and their two sons in southeast Iowa where he continues to write horror and science fiction short stories, as well as the novel-in-progress *E.R.A. - The Millennium War*.

Li-Ann Wong is a Global Nomad who currently majors in Law and Commerce at Macquarie University in Sydney, Australia. Amongst other things, she is a bibliophile, jazz cat, dessert addict, hopeless romantic... and almost 22!

Mercedes M. Yardley wears a bracelet made of silver stars.

Madam Z loves six and isn't afraid to admit it.

Claire Zulkey lives in Chicago and roots for the White Sox. She edits the *MBToolBox* blog, a resource for freelancers operated by mediabistro. She is getting her Master's in Creative Writing from Northwestern University, and has had her work featured in *The Chicago Tribune*, *ElleGirl*, *Glamour*, and *Modern Bride*. (Anderson Cooper once told her she was "kempt" -- as opposed to "un.")

Author Blogs and Websites

Nicole Andrea Aube
myspace.com/nicoleandreaaube

austere seeker
sixsentences.ning.com/profile/austere

Julian Baker
sybawrite.wordpress.com

Suzanne Baran
bigtakeover.com/author/Suzanne+Baran

David Barringer
davidbarringer.com

Diane Becker
notdesignedtojuggle.wordpress.com

Jeremy Blachman
jeremyblachman.typepad.com

Nathalie Boisard-Beudin
spacedlaw.blogspot.com

Ryan W. Bradley
ryanwbradley.blogspot.com

Paul D. Brazill
pauldbrazill.blogspot.com

Georgina Bruce
thebeardedlady.wordpress.com

Salvatore Buttaci
sixsentences.ning.com/profile/SalvatoreButtaci

Elissa Cain
sixsentences.ning.com/profile/elissa

Carolyn Carceo
sixsentences.ning.com/profile/Carolyn

Jeanette Cheezum
hamptonroadswriters.org

Peter Cherches
petercherches.blogspot.com

Robert Clay
bob-clay.co.uk

Christopher Cocca
christophercocca.wordpress.com

Linda Courtland
sixsentences.ning.com/profile/LindaCourtland

Craig Daniels
washthebowl.com

Tess Dickenson
sixsentences.ning.com/profile/TessDickenson

Emily Anne Epstein
emilyanneepstein.com

Thom Gabrukiewicz
thomg.blogspot.com

Timothy Gager
timothygager.com

Mel George
thepygmygiant.wordpress.com

Eugenia E. Gratto
100proofstories.com

Melody Gray
writetoday.wordpress.com

Rachel Green
leatherdyke.co.uk

Amy Guth
guthagogo.com

Christine Hamm
chamm.blogspot.com

Paige L. Hanson
sixsentences.ning.com/profile/PaigeLHanson

Zeptimius Hedrapor
snowstone.com

Sean Patrick Hill
theimaginedfield.blogspot.com

Peter Holm-Jensen
notesfromaroom.com

Tim Horvath
timhorvath.com

Prachi Jain
sixsentences.ning.com/profile/PrachiJain

Rebecca Jane
rjaneflashfiction.blogspot.com

Keturah Jones
sixsentences.ning.com/profile/TooraLee

Jason Jordan
decompmagazine.com

Lakin Khan
lakinkhan.blogspot.com

Eric Kramer
creamyiraq.blogspot.com

Tara Lazar
anonymom.wordpress.com

Heather Leet
poetryfromxegbp.blogspot.com

Tao Lin
heheheheheheheeheheheehehe.com

Joe Lo Truglio
joelotruglio.com

Jodi MacArthur
jodimacarthur.blogspot.com

Donna Martines
donnamartines.synthasite.com

Doug Mathewson
little2say.org

Hosho McCreesh
nyqpoets.net/poet/hoshomccreesh

Robert McEvily
sixsentences.blogspot.com

Peggy McFarland
sixsentences.ning.com/profile/peggy

Doug McIntire
dougmcintire.com

Kevin Michaels
myspace.com/kmwriter

Lisa Miller
sixsentences.ning.com/profile/LisaMiller

Rick Moody
myspace.com/fairuseinc

Mindy Munro
butterfliesonpins.typepad.com

Amy Sue Nathan
amysuenathan.com

Jillian Parker
myspace.com/flameinthesnow

Whitney Pastorek
whittlz.com

Jessica Patient
writerslittlehelper.blogspot.com

Pamila Payne
vintagevice.com

Juliana Perry
mythreeminions.blogspot.com

Kate Pilarcik
absolutelykate.blogspot.com

Sherrie Pilkington
hamptonroadswriters.org

Lisa Reynolds
reynoldsfitness.tripod.com

Fiona Rebeiro
fionakillackey.com

Ian Rochford
ionplayer.blogspot.com

Harry B. Sanderford
sixsentences.ning.com/profile/Harry

Oceana Setaysha
setaysha.blogspot.com

Emily Sheer
unicornshoes.blogspot.com

Tracy Shields
sevenperfumes.wordpress.com

Tovli Simiryan
mysite.verizon.net/vzeej44z

Linda Simoni-Wastila
leftbrainwrite.blogspot.com

James Simpson
jamessimpson.wordpress.com

Ben Spivey
yourbrainsblackbox.blogspot.com

Brian Steel
brian66.com

Daniel Stine
sixsentences.ning.com/profile/Daniel

Belinda Subraman
belindasubraman.com

Sondra Sula
sondrasula.imagekind.com

Kelley A. Swan
kelleyaswan.com

Kim Tairi
angelshavethephonebox.wordpress.com

Nicole Taylor
sketchmediahouse.wordpress.com

Doug Wacker
drinklings.googlepages.com

David Wain
davidwain.com

Caroline Wells
sixsentences.ning.com/profile/CarolineWells

Maggie Whitehead
dontforgettodance.com

Adam J. Whitlatch
TheBloodRaven.com

Mercedes M. Yardley
abrokenlaptop.wordpress.com

Madam Z
z-to-u.blogspot.com

Claire Zulkey
zulkey.com

Flip back to page 257. It turns out "The Invisible Six" isn't so invisible after all. It's actually a hidden message. If you'd like to know what it says, send an email to sixsentences at yahoo dot com. Make sure your subject line reads "The Hidden Message." You'll be glad you did.

What can *you* say in six sentences?

sixsentences.blogspot.com